Matters
of the
Heart

Matters of the Heart

Juanita Bynum, Ph.D.

Charisma®
HOUSE

MATTERS OF THE HEART by Juanita Bynum, Ph.D.

Published by Charisma House

A part of Strang Communications Company

600 Rinehart Road

Lake Mary, Florida 32746 ·

www.charismahouse.com

Unless otherwise noted, all Scripture quotations are from the Amplified Bible. Old Testament copyright © 1965, 1987 by the Zondervan Corporation. The Amplified New Testament copyright © 1954, 1958, 1987 by the Lockman Foundation. Used by permission.

Scripture quotations marked KJV are from the King James Version of the Bible.

Scripture quotations marked NIV are from the Holy Bible, New International Version. Copyright © 1973, 1978, 1984, International Bible Society. Used by permission.

Cover design by Judith McKittrick
Interior design by David Bilby

Library of Congress Catalog Card Number: 2002110340

International Standard Book Number: 0-88419-832-4

03 04 05 06 07 — 12 11 10 9 8 7

Printed in the United States of America

To Mother Estella Boyd:

Thank you for the impartation of the new heart message.

Contents

Preface

If you believe in God, you already know that we are entering a new era. Things have stepped up in the third realm, and they are rapidly changing on earth. If you listen to God and have felt the "temperature" of the spirit realm steadily rise, this book will confirm to you what He has already spoken.

> O Judah, and ye inhabitants of Jerusalem; Believe in the LORD your God, so shall ye be established; believe his prophets, so shall ye prosper.
>
> —2 CHRONICLES 20:20, KJV

Hear me. It is time to seek God like never before. It is time to fall down at the altar and ask Him to renew your heart. It is time to become more like Jesus, *for real.* "Church as usual" is over. It is time to take off the "old wineskin" and put on the "new man." (See Matthew 9:16–17; Colossians 3:9–10.) God has been walking me through this process for several years.

As I began to write this book, I realized that I could only "birth" chapters as the Holy Spirit moved me—and say only what He had given me to say. So as you read on, understand that this is a work of the Spirit. God wants you to know that He is breathing a message through His prophet for this hour.

This birthing has been difficult, sometimes painful,

so I know it will not be easy for you to read or to digest. Why? It is spiritual "meat." It takes more "energy" to digest meat in the natural, and it is no different in the realm of the Spirit. You will have to work through the revelation, just as God led me to do. So take your time, chew every piece, and let it go down deep—because by the time you finish, a "new" work will have begun inside of you.

A Work of Obedience

In Acts 5:29 we read: "We must obey God rather than men."

Peter and the other apostles said this to the high priest after being arrested for preaching the gospel in Jerusalem and then being supernaturally set free by the angel of God. The religious leaders were perplexed, and they commanded the apostles never again to preach in Jesus' name. The apostles stood their ground. God had prepared them for that day. They had learned from walking with Jesus and were empowered by the Holy Spirit. Under intense persecution, they boldly stood for what God had called them to do. I have come to this same realization. If you let this Word go deep, so will you.

The prophetic call in this book will not "tickle" your ears. As a matter of fact, your flesh could become uncomfortable or even flare up before you discover the Truth that will set you free (John 8:32). Watch out! This Word is not meant to please the status quo or the religious elite. It is a Word for this hour, for those who are ready to *get real* with God—

and themselves. If your heart has been crying out for more, then get ready to move to the next level.

It takes more "energy" to digest meat in the natural, and it is no different in the realm of the Spirit.

Church, as we have known it, is over. Without realizing it, we have fallen into error—even while we have continued to do "good" things for God. We have tripped, stumbled and fallen in doing what He requires. Now God is sounding the charge. He is calling us to get back up:

> For a righteous man falls seven times and rises again, but the wicked are overthrown by calamity.
> —PROVERBS 24:16

God is crying out:

> Remember then from what heights you have fallen. Repent (change the inner man to meet God's will) and do the works you did previously [when you first knew the Lord], or else I will visit you and remove your lampstand from its place, unless you change your mind and repent.
> —REVELATION 2:5

Righteous one, God is calling you to turn! Get up, turn around and start walking in a new direction. God is calling for change from the inside out, whether you minister from the church platform, work in the nursery or sit in the pew. Change is necessary for all of God's people. Whether you are a pastor, lay minister, church member or missionary, God wants you to "divide" this Word, first to yourself, and then to others.

I have come to this same realization. If you let this Word go deep, so will you.

This book will give you revelation, information and inspiration to do just that. When you get to the scientific chapter on the heart, for example, you are going to be amazed at what God has already done inside of you! You will either shout "Hallelujah!" or fall to your knees. One way or the other, you are going to learn a few things that even I have never heard taught *anywhere* before. Then you will know exactly where you stand with God and how you have been built to walk in His ways. The choice is yours.

As you read, God will deposit something "new" inside of you if you ask for it. Receive and embrace this Word. Receive this prophetic call, and God will bless, strengthen and guide you in the days to come. Your heart will begin to turn in a new direction… and, like me, you will know that you can never turn back.

> Therefore if any person is [ingrafted] in Christ (the Messiah) he is a new creation (a new creature altogether); the old [previous moral and

> spiritual condition] has passed away. Behold,
> the fresh and new has come!
>
> —2 CORINTHIANS 5:17

It is time to let go of the past. Let go of religion. Let go of sin and anything that keeps you from drawing close to God and obeying His prophetic cry for this final hour.

Read on, and enter the new day.

Introduction

How It **All Began**

It happened unexpectedly. I knew that I was saved—born and raised in the church for that matter—so why was God birthing this "new heart" message in me? Didn't He know to whom He was talking? I had grown up in the ministry and then moved on into my own full-time ministry, so I was used to the routine. Certain things were just part of my personality...had been for many years. I didn't realize it at that moment, but it was time for a change.

Many of God's people think the way I thought. We assume that we operate from our personalities, that we have a certain style—a *modus operandi*—when really, it is a much deeper matter. In actuality, our preconceived thought patterns move us far away from God's character and from what He expects from us as His children.

It was difficult for me to receive this message about a new heart. I already had a major "platform" and was in the public eye. But that did not matter to God. Though it was painful and slow, I had to begin taking that deep, inner look. I needed to "internalize" my walk with God.

So many of us want to concentrate our efforts on our "overt" walk with the Lord, one where we are more interested in what others think than we are with what God thinks about us. We constantly try to "fix up" what people see about us.

Right before we held the Chicago Summit in May of 2000, God confronted me with this "new heart" message, and I ended up preaching it then—and since. Before the Chicago conference, we had held a summit in Pensacola, Florida—which did not turn out the way that I thought it should have. We had rented a ten-thousand-seat auditorium, and only about six to seven thousand attendees showed up. But it wasn't just the attendance; across the board the conference did not turn out the way that I had hoped. Immediately after that conference, I started carrying a burden—Pensacola had been unsuccessful.

As the date approached for the Chicago Summit, the Lord began to get my attention. We were planning to have the event in a beautiful church that seated forty-five hundred people. It was going to be impressive. You see, I was determined, because of what had "happened" in Pensacola, that I was going to make the Chicago Summit go over the top—everything was going to be just right.

Then I was hit with the unexpected. A couple of days before the conference, we ran into difficulties with the building and had to switch to another facility. It was not as big and was more difficult for the people to get to. As we made the last-minute switch, I found myself, again, going into turmoil. How could this happen? We had been fasting and praying for this meeting!

God began to deal with me. He started showing me that my "burden" was not for the people and what I felt they would receive. I was more concerned for *my image*, what I would project and what others were going to "read it" to be. I shut down. As I prayed, I remembered the day that my assistant, Tonya, had called me. Just as I pulled up to my garage, the phone rang and she explained why we were not going to be able to use the "beautiful" facility. When she was finished I hung up and began to weep.

As the tears rolled down my face, God said, "You are thinking like man. You are always concerned about the outward appearance. You are always trying to make that outward image look acceptable." He continued, "Jesus made Himself of no reputation… yet it is your reputation that has become most important to you. You are thinking about all that you are doing, the major platforms where you are able to speak and all the exposure that you are getting. But what is the condition of your heart toward Me and toward My people?"

I sat there in my driveway, confused, and said to the Lord, "My heart…? You know that everything I am doing, I am doing to please You."

He responded, "You are not doing what you can to please Me. You are doing what you can to please people. You are doing what you can to be accepted by people, so they can say, 'Oh, Juanita Bynum is really successful. Oh, she did a conference…'"

Then He began to show me how my burden for the Pensacola Summit was not really about whether the people had or had not been blessed. They were blessed. But the truth was that I had left that conference wondering, *What are people going to say because the auditorium was not filled? What are people going to say because this or that thing was not right? What are people going to say because the flyers looked homemade?*

God said, "Let Me show you some little things...," and He started surfacing things about my personality, things I had reasoned were "just me"—but really, they were errors in my heart. He said, "The sad thing is, you are so far away from Me. You are nowhere near Me, though you think that you are."

He took me to Ephesians 2:8, which says that we are not saved "by works." Then He continued, "You need to accept the fact that I am making you the 'righteousness of God.' You have been working under the assumption that all of your works have impressed Me, and *I am not impressed by any of it.*"

Finally He said, "The reason that I am not impressed is because you are so far away from the goal that I have set for you. You are racing, trying to 'make it happen' on a big scale in auditoriums and all of that. But what about the little, everyday people whom I put on your heart to be a blessing to? You have ignored *that* because you think nobody can see it."

God dealt with me as I sat there in my driveway. He said, "I want to give you a new heart."

"A new heart?" I asked. "But I already feel like I am saved."

"Your salvation is according to the salvation of the traditional church," He responded. "Now, I want to save you *for real.*"

A Real Conversion? A True Salvation?

I was not expecting to receive a "new heart" message. I felt that I had given my heart to God when I was converted, but somewhere along the way it had gone into a dormant state. I began to operate from my "works," not from my heart. I am not even sure that I can explain or make sense of it, but I will try.

God saves and converts your spirit, which is where your heart is. Your mind, on the other hand, resists being transformed. If your mind is not transformed, then the miracle "heart" that God has placed in you will never be able to manifest in your lifestyle. This is because your mind, which is comprised of your soulish emotions and intellect, wants to run and rule. When the new heart is neglected, the mind assumes control through the old, carnal nature. That is what happened to me.

I knew that I had accepted Christ as my personal Savior. My spirit man, or my heart, was converted, and I began to get into the Word. You see, I wanted to transform my mind so that my life could begin to experience what had happened in my heart. Then somewhere along the line, I started reading the Word of God to prepare me to preach the gospel—not to convert my own mind.

When I began doing this, even though I was preaching a powerful gospel, I was having difficulties and struggles in my personal life, constantly warring against the flesh. My mind warred against my heart, and my heart warred against my mind. I could never seem to bring my thoughts and emotions under subjection to my converted heart.

My ministry became my career, and even though I knew that I had been called to preach, I believe it was God's compassion for His people that kept me there. Hear me. When God's people cried out in the Old Testament, He would supply what they needed because He had heard their cry. His heart is tender toward His people. So when I said to Him that I was willing to "go," and there was a cry from His people, He anointed me and used me in His work.

Yet God loved me so much that He said, "While you are preaching to others, I do not want to forget about you."

The True Heart Revealed

The Lord took me to Jeremiah 17:9–10, where He said:

> The heart is deceitful above all things, and it is exceedingly perverse and corrupt and severely, mortally sick! Who can know it [perceive, understand, be acquainted with his own heart and mind]? I the Lord search the mind, I try the heart, even to give to every man according to his ways, according to the fruit of his doings.

God had tried my heart, and I had failed the test. As a result, in all the good that I was doing, my heart still wore the core of wickedness.

If we are not careful, we can be doing a religious work and still be backslidden in our hearts. We can do this without realizing it, either because our works are so *wonderful* or because the responses our works are getting are so *wonderful*. We may even feel God's anointing and presence upon our works, which can, in itself, become a deception. How? Our works can be so "good" that we never stop to recheck our heart to see if it is found in right standing with God.

Regardless of everything I do—the preaching, the singing and all of the ministering—I am still human just like anyone else. Recently God told me, "I want you to turn off the music...turn off all the preaching tapes...be alone with yourself and see what comes out of your mind. Then you will know what state you are in. If you do this, you will be surprised what you hear yourself saying."

I had to be honest with myself and realize that my heart was not right. What I really said to myself, and what is hard for me to say even now, is, "Am I really saved?" I am not talking about a "hallelujah" experience. I had to ask, *"Am I really saved? Does Jesus really live here?* Am I sure, beyond the shadow of a doubt, that He lives in me? I do not have any doubt that He uses me...but does Jesus live here? Am I His?"

As God began to minister to me about a new heart, He took me to John 10:24–26, which says:

> So the Jews surrounded Him and began asking Him, How long are You going to keep us in doubt and suspense? If You are really the Christ (the Messiah), tell us so plainly and openly. Jesus answered them, I have told you so, yet you do not believe Me [you do not trust Me and rely on Me]. The very works that I do by the power of My Father and in My Father's name bear witness concerning Me [they are My

credentials and evidence in support of Me]. But
you do not believe and trust and rely on Me
because you do not belong to My fold [you are
no sheep of Mine].

It was like I experienced an awakening. The Lord
said, "Do you not know that when you constantly
walk in rebellion to the things that I tell you to do…
and the things that I say *no* to…and things you know
I am displeased with…and you keep doing it, contin-
uing in that way, that is when you have to ask yourself, 'Am I really His?'"

When I heard God tell me that, I remembered
John 10:4–5, which, in essence says, "My sheep
know My voice, and a stranger they will not follow."

The Lord continued speaking to me, saying, "If you
continue to go in this direction and to think that way,
then I cannot be there. I can't be there if you continue to think that everybody owes you something. If
you respond to others by thinking, *Oh, these people
offended me. I can't stand that one. I do not like her.
I am not speaking to this one over here,* I cannot be
there. If you travel all over the country, yet continue
to feel that way, I won't be there. I am not talking
about a sporadic thought pattern—I am talking about
that constant discord in your heart. If you continue
in that discord, then I cannot be there."

Hear this message that God gave to me. Sin and
God cannot dwell in the same heart at the same time.
Righteousness and unrighteousness cannot dwell in
the same temple. I am talking about your heart.
Thought patterns can emerge in your mind because
it has to be transformed. But when all the stuff that
goes on in your mind becomes a continuous rotation,

and it comes out in your behavior, then *are you really saved?*

We Must Receive a New Heart

You may wonder what happened at the point of conversion when you came up to the altar to be saved from your sinful nature. Was your heart truly converted? What happens to your heart at the moment of repentance?

We can look at the example of King David, a man after God's own heart. When he reached his moment of repentance and asked God to forgive him for his sins, he said, "Create in me a clean heart, O God, and renew a right, persevering, and steadfast spirit within me" (Ps. 51:10). That is exactly what took place right at that moment you asked Him to forgive you of your sins. He created a clean heart in you and renewed a right spirit within you. Within your heart your spirit *sits*.

It is your "old mind" that keeps you functioning outside of the will of God. Your mind needs to be transformed constantly by a process of renewing. (I will go into more detail about the renewing of your mind in chapter nine.)

In Romans 12:2 we read, "Do not be conformed to this world…" Whatever you do now, it should not conform to this world's way of thinking. In order to be transformed, you must renew your mind *every day*. When the renewed mind lines up with the conversion that is in your heart, you are a new creature—completely inside and out.

The only way your renewed mind can fail to come into harmony with your new heart is by your choice. You must choose whether to follow the stubborn habits that are stored in your memories or to submit to the wisdom that flows out of your new heart.

The most important thing is to have the new heart and to know that you know— *you have it.*

When God gave me that revelation as I sat in my car, I began asking, "God, give me a clean heart. Give me a new heart, right now. Save me all over again, right now. Save me, right here in this car, until I know that I am saved." I cried out, "Save me, Jesus!" just as I did when I first got saved.

Immediately, an old hymn came up in my spirit:

> Give me a clean heart, so I may serve Thee, Lord.
> Cleanse my heart, so that I may be used by Thee.
> Lord, I am not worthy of all these blessings,
> But give me a clean heart...[1]

A New Heart...a New Life

By the time I arrived in Chicago, everybody saw it— I was renewed. I was a new person. *Brand-new.* It was an experience that I had never had before in my Christian walk. I cannot put words to it. Suddenly, preaching, television, major platforms and all those wonderful things became secondary. Since May 2000, the first thing on my list has been making sure that everything I do pleases God. Now, for every thought pattern I ask, "Where did that thought come from?" If it is not a thought from my renewed mind, I say, "No! I rebuke that right now."

Since that life-changing encounter with God, I became the custodian of my own heart. Caring for my new heart is my major job right now.

Don't Be Lost in the Church

Since that time, I have also been compelled to give someone else the same opportunity—the opportunity to get saved *for real*. Yes, I mean it. God has birthed a "new heart" message in me!

Since it became my own experience, I have felt like I need to tell the world! I have to tell the nations what I found out. I have to tell the world about this new heart. I have to tell them that they must make sure they get it…that, above all—*everything*—it is vital to have this new heart. The most important thing is to have the new heart—and to know that *you have it*.

The scary thing is, I had gone a long time not knowing the state that I was in because my works were so wonderful. Every time I think about it, I am amazed how I could help others find the way to Christ while I was lost in the church! I shake when I think that I could have gone to hell from major platforms.

I want to make this clear. We must all come to a

place where we either admit that we do not have a new heart or that we have mastered the *act* of salvation and become the *great pretenders*. Let me give you an example. Suppose someone tells you, "When you are saved, you are supposed to love Sister Watermelon." So you speak to Sister Watermelon and hug her; you do the saved "act," but in your heart, you cannot stand her.

What has happened to the church across the board is that we have become men pleasers. We have taught each other to master the church "act." Everybody looks saved; we know how to act saved; we know how to do saved stuff; and we know how to project saved. But our hearts are far from it—we are not even close.

We think, *Now that I am sanctified, I do not want to be "looked down upon" or "scorned." I do not want to be out of relationship with my pastor, so I am going to come to church, "like he said."* But in reality, our hearts are far from the church—we are not even there.

A person who maintains the reins of his heart and controls the patterns of his mind impresses God.

We are the great pretenders. To all who fit into that category, one day Jesus will say: "You say you have cast out devils in My name and have healed the sick in My name—but begone from Me; I never knew you." (See Matthew 25:41.) *Don't let Him say that to you!*

What Jesus means is this: "I never had a relationship with YOU. You worked for Me, but I did not have a relationship with you."

One day Jesus' disciples came running back to Him, saying, "Lord, even the devils are subject unto us through thy name" (Luke 10:17, KJV).

Jesus replied:

> Rejoice not, that the spirits are subject unto you; but rather rejoice, *because your names are written in heaven.*
>
> —LUKE 10:20, KJV, EMPHASIS ADDED

Right from the beginning, Jesus was letting them know: "Do not get high about what happens in My name. You had better be high about the fact that your name is written in the Lamb's Book of Life." Right there, He set the priority. He said, "I am not impressed with spirits that are subject to you. All that you say you just did—great, but be impressed that you are saved. Then I am impressed." A person who maintains the reins of his heart and controls the patterns of his mind impresses God.

A New Birth…a New Mandate

God birthed the "new heart" message in me, and since that time, everything that I have preached on major platforms—anywhere that I have preached—I have *experienced* it. I have not experienced anything greater.

Everybody thought my book *No More Sheets* was an awesome message. It went to thousands, yes millions, of people. I preached that message because I had experienced it, but let me say again, I have not experienced anything greater than when God gave me a "new heart."

I have a mandate from God to preach this message. "A mandate?" you might ask. Yes, because I believe that of all the messages I have ever preached, this will be the greatest—regardless of whether or not it is recognized as such by man. The "new heart" was Jesus' greatest message. It is the Bible's greatest story. In all of Scripture, that with which God is most concerned is this vital truth—*the matters of the heart.*

Chapter 1

We Need a **New Heart**

Yes, we have a problem. Jeremiah 17 says that the heart is desperately wicked and "deceitful above all things... Who can know it" (v. 9). Yet before we can begin to look at this problem of the deceitful heart, we need to address another problem—an issue that has been part of Christendom for generations.

The Impossible Dream

God has brought me into relationship with a few secular people. In other words, they are not saved, and they do not go to church. They were, however, born and raised in the church. In my witnessing to them, one of them said to me, "We look over into Christendom and see either people who are very dogmatic about what they believe or who are so shallow in their beliefs that it is hard to accept that God can stabilize a person's life."

That surprised me. I was amazed, first, that he would even say it, and second, that he had made a valid point. Then this gentleman made a statement

1

that knocked me off my feet: "If you can find a way," he said, "if somebody in Christendom can find a way to make living for God attainable and reachable, then you do not know how many people would come to Christ."

I do not believe his standpoint was that the church should teach mediocrity. It struck a note inside of me concerning the Word that God had spoken to me about the new heart. While we were talking, I began to reflect about this new heart, and I remembered the reason why God had prompted me to write this message.

Take Me Back...

I had first heard about the new heart from Mother Estella Boyd, a powerful woman of God from Detroit. A lot of people know Mother Boyd and how powerful she is in the Spirit. There are times that she would say "deep" things, things that would scare me, because she ministers and speaks revelation from the third realm.

One night I was in a church meeting that Mother Boyd was leading. On this particular night, we were in one of those "afterglow" services (that is what we call it when we have had church and the power of God has fallen, leaving everyone kneeling and prostrate all over the place, praising God and wiped out—lying there in the presence of the Lord or sitting still in His presence), Mother Boyd spoke out, "We gonna be alright when we get that new heart." Half of us were on the floor or resting in the pews, clothing disheveled and hair out of place after persevering in worship during the service that night. It was unsettling to hear Mother Boyd telling us that we needed a "new heart" and that we would be all right when we got it. It was five years ago that Mother Boyd spoke that Word, and it has never left my spirit.

At some point I stored it away in the deep part of my mind, thinking to myself, *You know what? That is deep.* When I was first saved I believed that if I just kept working at it—kept letting God do what He was going to do in me—eventually, He would "fix" my heart. So I had learned to stash away such revelations deep within my mind so God could somehow just use that information to do His "fix" on me.

Mother Boyd's words about the new heart had really stung me, and they were always there in my mind, just deep enough that I never forgot them. Yet I never acted upon them. Then after my experience in Chicago in May of 2000, I started "guarding" my heart. But I did not begin to pursue the "new heart" until almost a year later, sometime around January 2001.

That day when the gentleman suggested to me that people were looking for a God who was attainable and reachable, I asked myself, "Is God attainable?" I realized I could not answer that question. But I stood there trying to figure out how and why the Lord had brought back to my memory His earlier message to me as I sat in my driveway about the "new heart."

Why is this happening? I thought. I did not understand exactly what the Lord was doing.

Time to Walk Out the Problem

I began to question God about this new heart. I felt strange, like some kind of cancer was eating away at me, something that I could not shake off. I knew that I was getting some signals from God. Not only would I preach this message—I was about to learn how to "walk it out."

I realized that since the night I first heard Mother Boyd speak about a new heart, I had felt as if I were falling all over myself trying to understand what she meant. I had to come to terms with God and with myself.

I started to observe people in ministry. I looked at the church—perfectly structured. I saw the choirs dressed in beautiful robes and the praise and worship teams with their matching outfits. One pastor would have on a nice, Versace suit and tie, and his wife would be sitting there with a St. John knit on—it all looked so perfect. It oozed "spiritual perfection" to the point that it became a problem for me.

The more I looked at the *problem*, the more I was forced to turn around and look within myself at my own situation. "OK, Juanita," I said to myself, "what is your problem? What is it that bothers you about this *so-called* walk with the Lord?" I began to examine this, and I remembered the lives of people who had stood before me throughout the years. I almost felt like a mouse that was chasing a piece of cheese, one it will never catch because it is tied to a cat's tail. That cat was running me all over the building! I could smell the cheese; I could come near the cheese; but I could never get a grip on the cheese because the cat was always moving.

So I said, "What is *my* problem?" I realized that through the years my problem had been my own feelings of spiritual inadequacy. I would look at my spiritual superiors and think to myself, *I can never become that. I can never be like Mother Boyd. I cannot ever be like Bishop Stacks. I could never be like the many people that God has placed in my life as spiritual examples.* I felt that I could never be like them because they were the epitome of spiritual perfection. Their status, to me, was *unattainable*.

When we pursue the "image" of perfection, we cannot strive to understand the heart of God.

Once I started my ministry, God helped me to realize the error of my heart. People began to come up to me and say, "Prophetess Bynum, you are such a blessing." "Prophetess Bynum, you have really blessed my life. You are such a woman of God."

Yet during that time there were areas in my life where God was still dealing with me. God was breaking some things in me and breaking other things *off* me. In other people's sight, my own image had become *unattainable*, but that was not reality. God began dealing intensely with me about my need to preach the "new heart" message.

If we consistently paint a picture that everything is perfect, beautiful and wonderful—"You know you have reached God when you look like me…dress like me…walk and talk like me"—then we have totally missed God! We have become a group of people who constantly pursue an image—not God! Is this reality? When we pursue the "image" of perfection, we cannot strive to understand the heart of God.

Who is trying to understand what God requires of us? Who is trying to understand that our life in Christ, though part of Christendom, is founded on an individual relationship that each one of us must have with the Lord…alone?

The Brain Has Assumed Control

When I began to understand the basic truth God was birthing in me about the new heart, I started to understand that the heart is "desperately wicked."

We are all struggling in our own way, trying to make sure that we "do right" from our heart. Through my study, I discovered that this world has become a brain world. It functions from the activities of the brain, out of the intellect of our finite brains. We are consumed with brain knowledge, and because we are consumed with this knowledge, our lives are constantly being constructed and operated by the laws of the intellect. What that means is this: If you do me wrong, then my intellect (based on the information that I have gathered from you) reacts and says, "I am going to do you wrong."

The brain teaches us how to scheme, lie, connive and manipulate. Here is the truth. God has put a spirit of conviction in our hearts, which corrects us when we do something wrong. The world, however, has trained us to bypass our heart's conviction and to operate within the realm of our mind and emotions. For this reason, we have a chaotic world.

This is also the reason why no one is seeking after God for a changed, *new heart*. We do not want to change; we only want to feel better—for the moment. In order to get *eternal* gratification, we have to give up something *right now*.

My mother used to say, "You know that you are growing when you give up your right to 'be right.'" You are maturing when you are the first to apologize, the first to keep the peace, when you are the first to say, "What did I do wrong?" rather than nailing the other person to the wall for what they did to you. You evaluate yourself and say, "What did I do to that person? Was there something that I did to provoke his or her response?" When you look at the issue this way, then you can overcome a situation that has stagnated our society.

> In order to get *eternal* gratification, we have to give up something *right now*.

Everybody is moved by their emotions through their *logical* minds, which always look out for "Number 1." Emotions and logic react to the "threats" they perceive around them—everybody else is always wrong. This is how the "old heart" rules. It is the reason power struggles are so prevalent in our world.

What Does the Bible Say About It?

The Bible says that we are born in sin and shaped in iniquity (Ps. 51:5). We are born with an "old heart" nature that is already *coated* with the potential to do wrong. When we come into the world, our hearts are already shaped for this sin.

Iniquity is anything you do that God is not in. It is anything done against the will of God or against the laws or nature of God. If something is contrary to His character, it is iniquity. You have been shaped in that area by what society has taught you.

Because your heart is composed of the potential to sin, your mind is gradually trained to become a professional sinner. When your heart and mind "match up" in the spirit, then you have the heart described in Jeremiah 17:9 as "desperately wicked" (KJV). It is desperately deceitful…who can know it? Who can understand the depths of that heart?

How do I know that what I am saying is correct? In Deuteronomy 8:11–14 we read:

> Beware that you do not forget the Lord your God by not keeping His commandments, His precepts, and His statutes which I command you today, lest when you have eaten and are full, and have built goodly houses and live in them, and when your herds and flocks multiply and your silver and gold is multiplied and all you have is multiplied, then your [minds and] hearts be lifted up and you forget the Lord your God, Who brought you out of the land of Egypt, out of the house of bondage.

When you look at our society, you see that this is true—and I am not just talking about the secular world; I am talking about the church! We are in church, dancing and shouting and speaking in tongues, yet we have hearts of iniquity just like the world. How do I know this? Our barns are filled, our flocks are fed, our herds are gathered, and we have multiplied. We have built houses, and we have multiplied our strength. Our silver has been multiplied, our gold has been multiplied, and now our minds and our hearts are lifted up—against God and against each other—full of pride. We have forgotten the Lord.

It took the disaster of September 11 to bring a "seek" back into this country. It took this attack and the fear of ongoing terrorist attacks from another country to bring us to our knees. It took this incident to help us realize that in spite of all the cars, houses and everything we have, we need the Lord. Before September 11, our hearts and minds had left the Lord. We were not seeking Him. When we walk with hearts that are "shaped in iniquity," hearts that are born into sin, seeking the Lord is not important in them. This kind of heart does not come with a "Yes, Lord," in it.

What Is Our First Priority?

We have a people and a church society that are doing everything they possibly can to walk in the ways of God. But Deuteronomy 10:12 says that there is no way to walk in the ways of God unless you fear the Lord and love Him "with all thy heart and with all thy soul" (KJV).

In this scripture the word *soul* indicates all of your mind and all of your emotions.[1] Thus you cannot walk in God's ways unless you fear Him as God—with a fear unto obedience, not a fear that tries to escape Him—a fear that submits to Him, totally and completely. Above this, you cannot walk in His ways unless, *number one*, you love Him from the center of your being, your heart.

When you say, "I love You, Lord," but still walk in your own ways, then you do not really love the Lord.

So how can this "old heart," which was "born in sin" and "shaped in iniquity," love God? Real love cannot come out of this heart. Only a *phileo* kind of love (which means the natural human affection, with its strong feeling, or sentiment) can come from a wicked heart.[2] *Agape* love (unconditional and eternal) is never found in our "old hearts." The only way that you can truly love God is to love Him with the same love that He has given to you. It has to match in the third realm. You cannot love God from an earthly level, because God is eternal, and it can never work to love Him from an earthly perspective.

Anything that is of the earth is temporal. That is why 2 Corinthians 4:18 says, "...we consider and look not to the things that are seen...for the things that are visible are temporal..." Those things never last. We must look toward the things that are eternal, because only these things will endure throughout eternity. Whether you realize it or not, you have already been "built" to see the eternal—the choice is yours.

Loving God brings about a commitment to Him. When you love somebody, you are committed to him in every way. There is nothing that you will not do for someone you love. You would be willing to lay down your life for your loved one. So when you say, "I love You, Lord," but still walk in your own ways, then you do not really love the Lord. You are still going about in your "religious affairs," and you do not have a real relationship with Him, which will bring about a change of character and a change in the way you walk. A real relationship with Him enables you to walk in His commandments.

If you do not have a real relationship with Him, then you merely "appreciate" Him for the life and breath that He has given you. You are grateful for the way He makes for you out of no way and for all the things He permits you to have. But you are still operating from a materialistic standpoint—and that is not real love. It cannot become real until you become committed and submitted to *His ways*.

The Deception of Prosperity

We must learn to deal with the deception of prosperity. We can find ourselves saying things like this: "I feel so much love for the Lord because of all the things He has blessed me with." Beware of the deception that can come with the prosperity of God's blessing upon our lives. God told the children of Israel:

> And you shall [earnestly] remember all the way which the Lord your God led you these forty years in the wilderness, to humble you and to prove you, to know what was in your [mind and] heart, whether you would keep His commandments or not.
>
> —DEUTERONOMY 8:2

God has allowed us to look upon the example of the children of Israel in the wilderness so that we could learn from their experiences. Just as He needed to humble the Israelites and create a spiritual hunger within them, so too He has "humbled" us and "allowed you to hunger" (v. 3). We see that God:

> ...fed you with manna, which you did not know nor did your fathers know, that He might make you recognize and personally know that man does not live by bread only, but man lives by every word that proceeds out of the mouth of the Lord.

I believe that God has allowed not just the secular world, but also the church, to go the "way" that we have gone to prove to us that we really do not love Him. He has done this to "try" us and to see what is really in our hearts and minds. The problem we face today, which is a huge problem and a mighty task, is that we, God's people, must ask for a new heart.

The problem becomes finding a people willing to do

this. We have to plow deeply into the church system to find people who are crying to God…a remnant sitting in the body of Christ in this hour that is willing to say, "I have to have the heart of God. I have to have a new heart. I have to be able to have a real relationship with God outside of the pews, outside of the choir roll, outside of my favorite preacher or evangelist. How do I get back to God—simply God?" Simply God, without all the props. Simply God, without all the drama. Where does this relationship start? How does it begin? What is the real purpose of your relationship with God?

The problem that we face today, which is a huge problem and a mighty task, is that we, God's people, must ask for a new heart.

Having taken a deep look at the church, the instrument God uses to draw people into His kingdom, I have to ask this question: How can the church do the work of the Spirit—not just the work of Christendom—to the point that she has the power to be as compassionate as Christ Himself? Where will we find the eternal love we need to embrace the kind of sinners who are coming to Christ in this hour? How can we work for God when our hearts are far from Him, when we do not know who He is?

The Deception of Religion
~◦~

As a prophet I look at Solomon's example and am concerned about the longevity of the church. If we, the church, do not make this switch—the switch from being a religious organization to having a relationship with our Father—in the twenty-first century, then we are going to fail in our efforts. We will not be able to accomplish what God has given us to do.

King Solomon inherited the kingdom of his father, David, and was handed the plans of the tabernacle that David had earnestly desired to build. Yet in 1 Kings 11:3, we discover that "…his wives turned away his heart from God." Even though he began his reign over Israel by seeking God's wisdom, and even though he built the temple of God, his kingdom became little more than a religious organization— and he lost his relationship with his Father God. We discover that he even followed his foreign, idolatrous wives into the worship of false gods, building temples of worship to these gods (v. 8). As a result:

> The Lord was angry with Solomon because his heart was turned from the Lord, the God of Israel.
>
> —1 Kings 11:9

King Solomon failed to receive his new heart. Just as it was with Solomon, I believe God's anger is kindled against us when He sees the way we are being drawn into worldly change, causing us to turn from Him and to begin walking in the way of the world around us.

Like Solomon we do not even realize that our

hearts are being drawn away. We may even say, "I've been religious all my life. Do I really need a new heart? Why would God be angry with me?" We may have walked closely with God in the past and, like Solomon, may have even prayed for His wisdom to guide our steps. Verse 9 goes on to tell us that God had already appeared to Solomon and commanded him that he should not go after other gods! However, Solomon did not do what the Lord had commanded. His disobedience kindled the anger of God:

> Therefore the Lord said to Solomon, Because you are doing this and have not kept My covenant and My statutes, which I have commanded you, I will surely rend the kingdom from you and will give it to your servant!
>
> —1 KINGS 11:11

This is a powerful revelation—one that carries great significance for us. God has been forewarning the church structure for many years, saying, "Get this thing together; get this thing in order. I want you to provoke My people to come after My heart, to provoke My people unto righteousness."

Even now, God is starting to put His Word into the mouths of people outside the church walls. People outside of the church "organization"—hippies, secular artists and others—are rising up and leading God's people! They were not born and raised in the church; they knew nothing about God, but through divine impartation God is teaching them. God is using these "slaves of this world," people functioning in a "servant's status," instead of the disobedient "sons and daughters" in organized religion.

We in the church have considered ourselves to be "structured" and "mighty." We think that we have all of the answers. We have an appearance of God—but because we have not turned our hearts toward Him, we are leaving Him with no option. We are leaving God with no other choice except to reach out, get the heathen and raise them up. They are the ones who have received the new heart. They are teaching people to come to Him.

This problem affects not only the church, but also the world. Like Solomon, many believers have prosperity in their own eyes. They have built mighty temples to God, just as Solomon had done. They have received the accolades of men. But it is at this very point of "self" success that the heart can be in its greatest form of deception.

Then the world cannot see Jesus, nor can people come to Him.

Why? Because, without realizing it, these leaders have come to expect others to praise their works. They have become people pleasers. They have forgotten that as God's children they have been called to carry the image of Christ—that of a servant to others.

> And whoever desires to be first among you must be your slave—just as the Son of Man came not to be waited on but to serve, and to give His life as a ransom for many [the price paid to set them free].
>
> —MATTHEW 20:27–28

When we forget that we are here to serve, not to be served, the cycle of deception is in full swing. Then the world cannot see Jesus, nor can people come to Him.

Yes, church, we have a problem...and this is just the beginning.

Chapter 2

We Have an
Inside-Out Problem

God continued to unfold His revelation about a new heart as He taught me about the training base for the spirit of iniquity—our brain. The brain is the "computer" that gathers data from the world into this "character training center."

As I examined the role our brain plays in turning our hearts from God, I began to understand why everyone in our society learns to blame his or her shortcomings and lifestyle on somebody else. The easiest thing for the mind to do is to push blame toward another person.

When confronted with our own wickedness, it is so easy for us to say, "Well, I am evil because this or that happened to me," or "I am this way because that thing happened to me." Let's take a closer look at the spiritual side of the brain's training center. Psalm 51:5 records David's words:

> Behold, I was shapen in iniquity; and in sin did my mother conceive me.
>
> —KJV

No matter how a person comes into this world, and even though that person may be "morally good," the nature of sin hovers over that person's heart because it operates within the cold, carnal nature.

The easiest thing for the mind to do is to push blame toward another person.

Sin is manifested and activated as a result of the information that is fed into our sin nature from the world, via the "old heart" and the brain. When that sin information reaches the heart, it connects with the cold, carnal area in the heart. There the brain rationalizes that information as being "acceptable." From this union of our old, carnal heart with our brain, we manifest that information as an act of sin. Thus we become "sinners." From this, we are shaped in iniquity, shaped and raised up to walk in an era of disobedience toward God.

Mark 7:16–18 says:

> If any man has ears to hear, let him be listening [and let him perceive and comprehend by hearing]. And when He had left the crowd and had gone into the house, His disciples began asking Him about the parable. And He said to them, Then are you also unintelligent and dull and without understanding? Do you not discern and see that whatever goes into a man from the outside cannot make him unhallowed or unclean...

What comes into you from the outside is not what makes you unholy! Mark continues his explanation by saying:

> And He said, What comes out of a man is what makes a man unclean and renders [him] unhallowed. For from within, [that is] out of the hearts of men, come base and wicked thoughts, sexual immorality, stealing, murder, adultery, coveting (a greedy desire to have more wealth), dangerous and destructive wickedness, deceit; unrestrained (indecent) conduct; an evil eye (envy), slander (evil speaking, malicious misrepresentation, abusiveness), pride (the sin of an uplifted heart against God and man), foolishness (folly, lack of sense, recklessness, thoughtlessness). All these evil [purposes and desires] come from within, and they make the man unclean and render him unhallowed.
>
> —MARK 7:20–23

Is this God's choice? No! In the Garden of Eden we chose our own destiny. (See Genesis 3:1–24.) The Book of James goes on to explain further.

> Let no one say when he is tempted, I am tempted from God; for God is incapable of being tempted by [what is] evil and He Himself tempts no one. But every person is tempted when he is drawn away, enticed and baited by his own evil desire (lust, passions). Then the evil desire, when it has conceived, gives birth to sin, and sin, when it is fully matured, brings forth death.
>
> —JAMES 1:13–15

Our Problem Is Inside Out

The world—and part of the church—is crying out, but our problem always seems to be someone else's fault. Before you will see your own need, you must be confronted—just as I was—with the reality of what God is saying. The problem is not what is entering your life from external sources. It is not the fault of what is taking place around you. Those things that come "at you" from external sources are merely identifying with something that is already in your heart.

If the outside "problem" finds a place of identification, a familiar spirit, inside of you, then you absolutely, no doubt about it, need to be transformed. You need the "new heart." Jeremiah 17:9 says, "The heart is deceitful above all things, and it is exceedingly perverse and corrupt and severely, mortally sick! Who can know it [perceive, understand, be acquainted with his own heart and mind]?"

> # The heart determines whether or not you enter the kingdom of God.

Is this verse talking about someone who deals with "little ill feelings" against someone else? What kind of heart is this verse talking about? Why is the church in the position now of not realizing we need a new heart? Why do we feel that by getting our outward appearance "right," we are getting some-where with God?

It is because man looks outside, but God looks within—at the heart. It is our hearts that God is coming back for—nothing else. The heart—not the mind—determines whether or not you enter the kingdom of God.

We should not be concerned with outer things. We should focus on what is inside. When we get the "inside" to line up with God's Word, we will change! God will give us a new heart, and this heart will begin to manifest on the outer man just as the old heart works from the inside out.

What Is Our Old Heart Like?

What about our old heart? Is it simply a "poor, little, confused, messed-up heart"? We can begin to under-stand the condition of our old heart by taking a closer look at Jeremiah 17:9.

> The heart is deceitful above all things, and it is exceedingly perverse and corrupt and severely, mortally sick! Who can know it [perceive, understand, be acquainted with his own heart and mind]?

In this verse the word *deceitful* means, "to mislead by a false appearance or statement; to trick." We must recognize, first and foremost, that *God* called the old heart "deceitful above all things." It does not matter how much you try…how many Bible studies you attend…or what Bible classes you take. I do not care

how many times you say, "If I can just go to church
and sing in the choir, everything will be all right."

No! Remember that this wicked heart not only
misleads people, it *misleads YOU.* This heart gives a
false appearance, not just to people, but also to YOU.
It makes you think, *Because I look right, I am right.*

But there is another definition for the word *deceitful* that startled me—it also means, "to be unfaithful." The saddest fact about this heart—and again,
shockingly so—is that it is "unfaithful." It can never
be dedicated to God. It can never keep a commitment. Maybe this is the reason why people constantly move in and out of relationships, or why the
divorce rate is so high. Perhaps it is the reason why
so many children are living in orphanages, or why
prostitution is rampant. Maybe it is even why is
there such a lack of integrity in the body of Christ.
This deceitful heart does not have what it takes to be
faithful to anything—God or man.

The word *perverse* means that this heart is "willfully determined *not* to do what is expected or
desired." It is "turned away from what is right, good
or proper." This heart already has a willful desire
built into its mechanism *not* to perform what is
expected or desired.

For example, when we teach or minister from the
Word of God and expect that, as a result, people will
behave in a certain way, we are appalled when they
do not walk in this light. We expect them to be different, but if the heart within them is like the heart
described in Jeremiah 17, it does not have the
capacity to be "penetrated" by the Word! It is
already full—of deceit! It comes with a built-in will

that says, "I will not yield to God. I will not obey the things of God." Rebellion is already part of the makeup of the old heart. The old heart's nature is to go in the opposite direction of where God has sent it.

So when this heart hears the Word of God, it sits dormant in the sanctuary. The mind may "hear" the Word, yet the heart remains unchanged. Why? You need a "new heart" to receive and walk in the ways of God!

> # This deceitful heart does not have what it takes to be faithful to anything— God or man.

The verse in Jeremiah also calls the old heart "perverse and corrupt and severely, mortally sick." Not just mortally sick—*severely*, mortally sick. The word *severely* means, "grave, critical or harsh." It is "of extreme, intense violence in character and nature." This heart destroys everything that it touches. It can act "seemingly" for a little while, but this heart eventually tears up relationships. It is harsh, not kind. This heart will lead you to your grave. It is a heart of detriment that will literally steal your life away.

Since its nature and character are violent, you cannot correct it. When confronting people with an "old heart," you can expect rebellion and a harsh and violent reaction—in both attitude and conversation.

The verse says, "Who can know it [perceive, understand, be acquainted with his own heart and mind]?" *Acquainted with his own heart...* When you look up the word *acquainted,* you will discover that this phrase means, "Who is familiar enough with his own heart to furnish it with knowledge?" This is powerful. Who knows the depths of his heart to the degree that he can furnish this heart with the knowledge it will take to walk toward God? No man does. God tells us in Jeremiah 17:10:

> I the Lord search the mind, I try the heart, even to give to every man according to his ways, according to the fruit of his doings.

What are these "doings"? I believe that as God searches the heart and mind, He is going to give us the fruits of the "doings" listed in Mark 7, those unclean things that come out of our old hearts. (See Mark 7:20–23.) Yes, we have a real problem.

The Insensitive Heart of Man

The Bible says in Matthew 13:15:

> For this nation's heart has grown gross (fat and dull), and their ears heavy and difficult of hearing, and their eyes they have tightly closed, lest they see and perceive with their eyes, and hear and comprehend the sense with their ears, and grasp and understand with their heart, and turn and I should heal them.

Ephesians 4:17 adds:

> So this I say and solemnly testify in [the name of] the Lord [as in His presence], that you must

no longer live as the heathen (the Gentiles) do in their perverseness [in the folly, vanity, and emptiness of their souls and the futility] of their minds.

The word *futility* means that worldly minds are "incapable of producing any result...ineffective, useless and unsuccessful." People who operate from their soulish realm, through their minds, are incapable of producing anything of eternal value.

Their moral understanding is darkened and their reasoning is beclouded. [They are] alienated (estranged, self-banished) from the life of God [with no share in it; this is] because of the ignorance (the want of knowledge and perception, the willful blindness) that is deep-seated in them, due to their hardness of heart [to the insensitiveness of their moral nature].
—EPHESIANS 4:18

Can you see what this is saying? These ignorant minds want knowledge, but only according to their own perception. They have chosen to be blind; it is deep-seated in them due to their "...hardness of heart [to the insensitiveness of their moral nature]."

The Word cannot penetrate a "hardened," insensitive heart. The only way this heart can live is by the "knowledge" of the mind, which takes us back to the fleshly information center, the brain.

Iniquity constantly feeds the "old heart" information from the earthly realm. This spiritually insensitive heart fails to discern the truth of the Word and sends this "new knowledge" on to the brain. In turn, the brain tries to rationalize, or figure out, the spiritual revelation. When it cannot, it rejects the Word and tosses it to the side. Sadly, nothing that has the "breath of life"—especially the Word of the Lord—is welcome in the hardened heart. In its partnership with the mind, this heart cannot be penetrated.

If we do not ask for and receive a new heart, deception spreads like a virus. What are the telltale signs of a diseased heart? Let us look at a few examples.

Soil Along the Roadside

> Listen to the [meaning of the] parable of the sower: While anyone is hearing the Word of the kingdom and does not grasp and comprehend it, the evil one comes and snatches away what was sown in his heart. This is what was sown along the roadside.
>
> —MATTHEW 13:18–19

How is the "evil one" able to snatch a Word that has been sown in someone's heart? He is familiar with the grounds. He (Satan) already knows that the Word is trying to penetrate that heart; he knows the base character of that heart does not have what it takes to absorb and to hold that Word. The enemy knows already that the Word is sitting in a heart that has been consumed by the spirit of perverseness.

Have you ever known somebody who heard the Word of the Lord and then tried to change its meaning in order to justify his sin? This is what happens when the old heart is in operation. Satan, already familiar with the ground within that heart because he lives and rules there, *projects* himself there because he does not have a home. He takes control of that ground because the heart is filled with all of the enemy's works. That heart is filled with his ungodly character, and he will not allow anything that is righteous and holy to remain there.

At the point the Word of the Lord tries to penetrate into that heart, holy things are illegally trespassing on the enemy's ground. He has taken possession of that old heart. Satan has "grounds" to operate anywhere that he gains a legal precedent. The earth realm is "legal" ground for Satan. This is why believers must walk in the Spirit.

Satan has authority to do things according to the flesh because this ground belongs to him! He is "the "prince of the power of the air" (Eph. 2:2). The worldly realm is his, but Satan has not been given authority over the spiritual realm.

If your heart is not "spiritual," God would say to you:

> For whoever has [spiritual knowledge], to him will more be given and he will be furnished richly so that he will have abundance; but from him who has not, even what he has will be taken away.
>
> —MATTHEW 13:12

Are you getting the revelation? God warns that if you do not walk in the Spirit (and the way to "walk" in the Spirit is to receive the "new heart" of the Spirit), then Satan can take anything righteous that hits those grounds. He has a legal right to cancel it! You have given the right to him. Your heart has become foreign ground.

Rocky Soil
~⌇~

> As for what was sown on thin (rocky) soil, this
> is he who hears the Word and at once welcomes
> and accepts it with joy.
>
> —MATTHEW 13:20

Emotionalism—are you seeing the revelation? Many people hear the Word and "accept it with joy." You can see it every Sunday in the church. People hollering back at the preacher...shouting, "Amen, preach it" all over the church. "Yet...," the Bible says:

> ...it has no real root in him, but is temporary
> (inconstant, lasts but a little while); and when
> affliction or trouble or persecution comes on
> account of the Word, at once he is caused to
> stumble [he is repelled and begins to distrust
> and desert Him Whom he ought to trust and
> obey] and he falls away.
>
> —MATTHEW 13:21

God is describing people who hear the Word, but there is no real heart penetration. There is no depth to where His Word can be planted. It floats around in the "emotional" realm, and when something else "exciting" charges these emotions in a different way and direction, the first Word is canceled out. The emotions, which are fleshly, take precedence at that moment over the Word of God. The Word does not reside in this heart, and it cannot find a resting place.

Thorny Soil

> As for what was sown among thorns, this is he
> who hears the Word, but the cares of the world
> and the pleasure and delight and glamour and
> deceitfulness of riches choke and suffocate the
> Word, and it yields no fruit.
>
> —MATTHEW 13:22

The Word of the Lord cannot be implanted into the old heart. In order for the Word of the Lord to penetrate and take root in our lives, we must have a new heart. We must unseat Satan from his throne in our lives. James 1:21 tells us how to do that:

> So get rid of all uncleanness and the rampant
> outgrowth of wickedness, and in a humble (gen-
> tle, modest) spirit receive and welcome the
> Word which implanted and rooted [in your
> hearts] contains the power to save your souls.

The Bible tells us that once we have that new heart, we are to:

> Be doers of the Word [obey the message], and
> not merely listeners to it, betraying yourselves
> [into deception by reasoning contrary to the
> Truth].
>
> —JAMES 1:22

People who do not have the "new heart" hear the truth and then start "betraying" themselves through deceit (reasoning). They rationalize that truth and come up with every reason why "this is not what the Bible means." Their hearts are so filled with the world and the things of the world that they are deceived into thinking they have all they need.

Don't allow the "world and the pleasure and delight and glamour and deceitfulness of riches" to "choke and suffocate the Word" when God attempts to penetrate your heart with it. Don't let these "good" things choke the Word out of your heart! That is perversion.

> For if anyone only listens to the Word without obeying it and being a doer of it, he is like a man who looks carefully at his [own] natural face in a mirror; for he thoughtfully observes himself, and then goes off and promptly forgets what he was like.
>
> —James 1:23–24

A pattern repeats throughout the Bible—we need a new heart. Why? Let us look at one example of a "good heart" to see what God desires.

Good Soil

> As for what was sown on good soil, this is he who hears the Word and grasps and comprehends it; he indeed bears fruit and yields in one case a hundred times as much as was sown, in another sixty times as much, and in another thirty.
>
> —Matthew 13:23

The person represented in this parable about the good soil has a converted heart. This person, who has received a new heart, has an "active" Word on the inside. God's spoken Word comes alive and produces good fruit. This Word has the power to save and the power to keep. How do I know it is operative? Hebrews 4:12 says:

> For the Word that God speaks is alive and full of power [making it active, operative, energizing, and effective]; it is sharper than any two-edged sword, penetrating to the dividing line of the breath of life (soul) and [the immortal] spirit, and of joints and marrow [of the deepest parts of our nature], exposing and sifting and analyzing and judging the very thoughts and purposes of the heart.

The penetrating Word is filled with power! It energizes your spirit, heart and soul as it accomplishes God's will. This Word can never be stagnated. It goes down into the intricate parts of the inner man and "dissects" everything it finds there. When the enemy comes in "like a flood," that Word knows how to swim. When the fire rages, that Word knows how to hold its breath. When the wind starts blowing, that Word is anchored. When the sun starts to blaze, that Word knows how to get in the shade—regardless of what life's temperature may be.

When the Word takes up residence in this heart, it operates with divine power and produces more fruit. This heart embraces the Word it has received and produces more than it has been given. The Word that goes into a "new heart" is active. It "identifies" with the divine nature of God and multiplies.

Spiritually Lazy "Prey" in the Pews

Let us return to the "old heart" and our text from
Ephesians chapter 4. Since it is not made up of
"good soil," this heart rejects the Word, and the
downward cycle continues:

> In their spiritual apathy they have become cal-
> lous and past feeling and reckless and have
> abandoned themselves [a prey] to unbridled
> sensuality.
>
> —EPHESIANS 4:19

What a horrible situation. The people about which
this verse is speaking have fallen prey to everything
that is moved by the "prince of the power of the air,"
everything that swings in society—strange and perverted sensualities that prey upon people who do not
have the new heart!

The Word that goes into a "new heart" is active. It "identifies" with the divine nature of God and multiplies.

Spiritual apathy has no built-in defense system;
nothing "foreign" can be shielded off. Spiritual
laziness leaves no other alternative but to live a
reckless existence! These people are "prey" to
"unbridled sensuality," eager and greedy to indulge
in every form of impurity that their depraved

desires suggest and demand.

Lazy people do not digest the Word; they do not have the ability to break it down. They are defenseless against the enemy's thrust into "unbridled sensuality." That is why we are appalled at what we see in this world—cloning of human beings, men changing their sex to become women, women becoming men—all kinds of degradation, because this world has become a prey.

When the church does not step over into the spirit realm and receive this "new heart," then we sit idly by and become prey to the enemy. That is why we see so much degradation in the church! Things that have never happened before in the body of Christ are coming up out of our deceived hearts.

Here is the problem: The church has been preaching the gospel, but we have not been preaching conversion. We have been ministering to people about where they need to be, but we do not have the power to get them to where they should be! We have been telling people what God is saying, but we do not have the anointing upon our lives to destroy the yoke of the devil so that they can be converted—the proper way—to receive a new heart so the Word can penetrate and produce.

People are sitting in churches like "prey" in the pews. We are sitting like rabbits that are waiting for the next lion or tiger to strike. We are like deer prancing in the wilderness, waiting for the next wild animal to attack us, and we have no defense! Though we have spiritual mothers and fathers, and though we have pastors, we still have no defense. Why? Because we have not yet received a new heart.

Therefore, we are open prey to the devil and whatever kind of spiritual sensuality that swings in the
atmosphere. We cannot help but to indulge.

We operate in our soulish realm. When our mind
hears the Word of God, we know that what we are
doing is wrong. We know that God is displeased.
According to the Word of God that we hear, we know
that we are hell bound. But we cannot stop the
downward spiral because the old heart is racing
toward every damnable sin.

The heart races to impurity because that is its
nature. My pastor often told us, "If you take a hog
out of the hog pen, put a white bow on it, get him all
clean and sit him in a white living room on a white
couch, the first time that hog sees slop, he is going to
run out of that house and back to the slop, because
that is his nature."

We try to dress people up in the church. We have
incredible stained-glass windows and the most beautiful churches the world has ever seen. But the
minute the body of Christ, the spiritually lazy people
resting in the pews, sees the devil's slop—sexual
impurities, lies and deceit—they run right back to it
because that is still their nature.

Our loving heavenly Father warned us about this
tendency in Ezekiel 11:14–18:

> And the word of the Lord came to me, saying,
> Son of man, your brethren, even your kindred,
> your fellow exiles, and all the house of Israel, all
> of them, are they of whom the [present] inhab-
> itants of Jerusalem have said, They have gone
> far from the Lord [and from this land]; there-
> fore this land is given to us for a possession.
> Therefore say, Thus says the Lord God:

> Whereas I have removed [Israel] far off among the nations, and whereas I have scattered them among these countries, yet I have been to them a sanctuary for a little while in the countries to which they have come. Therefore say, Thus says the Lord God: I will gather you from the peoples and assemble you out of the countries where you have been scattered, and I will give back to you the land of Israel. And when they return there, they shall take away from it all traces of its detestable things and all its abominations (sex impurities and heathen religious practices).

Listen closely. In this hour God is saying the same thing to us:

> And I will give them one heart [a new heart] and I will put a new spirit within them; and I will take the stony [unnaturally hardened] heart out of their flesh, and will give them a heart of flesh [sensitive and responsive to the touch of their God], that they may walk in My statutes and keep My ordinances, and do them. And they shall be My people, and I will be their God.
>
> —Ezekiel 11:19–20

What is the answer to the problem? We need a new heart.

Chapter 3

The Prophecy **Begins**

Y ou may wonder why God did not deal with
me personally concerning my need for a
new heart until this late date in my ministry. God did begin dealing with me long before I
really grabbed hold of His Word to me about my need
for a new heart.

I remember earlier times when the Lord spoke
deep inside of me, sometimes in the middle of the
night or during my prayer time, saying, "Juanita,
you need a new heart." But I did not understand. I
felt that I had it all together. I knew that there were
some things I had to deal with because of situations
that had been caused by past offenses. But I felt that
I had been "working with it."

We all have areas that have become our "strong-
holds." We consider these areas to be our "weaknesses," a term we have been taught by the preaching in this era and season of life.

The mass majority of teachings that I have heard
say, "Be encouraged," "It's OK," "That's your weak-
ness" and "God understands." By all means, the Lord
does understand. Yet I believe that when you have
been called to the office of a prophet and begin to seek

the Lord with intensity, you strive not simply to receive a Word from Him to deliver to people, but to receive a Word from the Lord for *you*.

When you hear a Word from Him, you begin to change "inside." You asked for a Word *for yourself*—one by which you can *live*.

Transforming Prayer

Several years ago, my life began to take a turn when God called me to pray at 5:00 A.M. each morning. I would go into prayer for others, but I found that I began to yearn for another level in God for myself. I began to seek the Lord for a new depth in Him, for the God of Abraham and the God of Jacob. I wanted the God of the Old Testament. During this time, I remember seeing manifestations of the Spirit and character of God in Africa. "God," I prayed, "I want a relationship with You so that I can believe You for anything. I want to know who You are beyond a shadow of a doubt."

As I sought the Lord with intensity, I began to change. One of the first scriptures I heard Him speak to me was Matthew 5:8:

> Blessed are the pure in heart: for they shall see God.
>
> —KJV

I had read this verse from the Beatitudes many times. As a "Sunday school baby," I was raised on the Beatitudes. As far back as I can remember, even when I was three or four years old, my mother took us to Sunday school. The Beatitudes were some of the first Bible truths that I learned.

As I began to seek the Lord, "Blessed are the pure in heart: for they shall see God" came alive in my spirit. How could this happen? Why would God take me back to when I first learned about Him? After years of walking with Him, I had come to understand that there are different levels of revelation. There is the "milk" level of the Word, which leads to learning the "bread" of the Word, and, finally, you are able to move up to the "meat" of the Word.

Though I had heard this scripture many times before, I believe that God was trying to reveal the "meat" of this Word to me, which was the revelation of it from the third realm. From this realm behind the veil, we encounter the divine presence of God. It is where we learn the fullness of His heart and instruction. This is how, I believe, the Lord allows us to know "of" Him. Our spiritual level of understanding is based on the position of our heart "with" Him.

As this Word of the Lord, "Blessed are the pure in heart...," settled in my spirit, I remembered that I had always interpreted it to say, "Blessed are the pure in heart: for one day, when we die and go to heaven, we shall see God." The Lord began to say to me, "I desire that your spiritual eyes see Me now, but the only way that I can reveal My mysteries to you is according to My Word...the mysteries not yet revealed to man."

In Jeremiah 33:3, God said, "Call to Me and I will answer you and show you great and mighty things."

The Lord further said to me, "I will show you secrets that have not yet been revealed to man. I will not reveal My secrets to those whose hearts and motives are not pure." Then He added, "If you want to see Me in a way that you have never seen Me before, then I am compelling you to get a new heart."

I tried to respond by saying, "Well…I am struggling, and I see some things…I know that everything in my heart is not right. God, I just want You to fix it." During this season of early morning prayers, God revealed to me that He had no desire to reconstruct and "fix" my old heart. His desire and purpose was to give me *a new heart.* Deep down, I knew that He was right. How did I know this? The Lord took me to Luke 6:45:

> The upright (honorable, intrinsically good) man out of the good treasure [stored] in his heart produces what is upright (honorable and intrinsically good), and the evil man out of the evil storehouse brings forth that which is depraved (wicked and intrinsically evil); for out of the abundance (overflow) of the heart his mouth speaks.

When I listened to the language that came out of my mouth and observed some of my actions, I began to face what I call "the truth of all truth." Some of those actions repeated themselves over and over again, even after much time in prayer about them. The truth I faced was that, like the apostle Paul said, after I had preached to others, I had become a castaway (1 Cor. 9:27). I sought the Lord even more intently and said, "God above everything…" I put my ministry, fame and television personality on the back burner. I said to God, "I do not care what comes and what goes. Most of all, I want to make sure that I am saved *for real.*"

A Revelation for the World

As the Lord continued to deal with me about the new heart, I knew that by the time for me to minister that Word, I would already have learned to "walk it out." At that time, I did not understand why I had a problem forgiving people who had offended me. I did not understand why I was praying, "God, You know that I am trying to forgive them, but it just seems like I can't."

He began to reveal to me that the "old heart" does not come with forgiveness in it. The old heart does not come with mercy. The old heart does not come with compassion. This heart is born to be unfaithful to God. It is born without submissiveness. The nature of this heart is to operate from a spirit of rebellion—everything is conditional. You may hear that the unconverted heart has "eternal" qualities, but this contradicts the Word of God.

"You must begin to reveal this Word to the world," He told me. "I am not giving you this truth so that you hide your hands and say to people, 'Everything is going good. Everything is OK.'"

It made me stand back and take a long look at what I thought I had known and understood for so long. On the exterior, you can look at the church and see megachurches springing up everywhere. Christian programs have high ratings on television. Overall, Christendom is beginning to gain a new-found respect in the world.

Even still, I had to stand back and ask, Are we gaining respect because we are preaching an

uncompromising gospel? Are we "crying loud" and
"sparing not"? Or is the respect we are starting to
enjoy coming to us because the church is becoming
very cosmetic? Have we taken on the "cloak" or
appearance of the world to such a degree that the
world feels comfortable coming to the God we preach
about? Are they coming to Him because the God we
preach, after all, does not require us to sell out?

This "relaxed" gospel does not require that we
lament, grab hold of the horns of the altar and travail
for the birthing of souls—the "true" birthing process
that happens when a soul comes through the birth
canal the proper way. Today's "religion" says, "Come
as you are and stay as you are. It is just between you
and God, because God understands." Watch out!
The Bible says that in the last days, the hearts of
men will "wax cold," and they will not "endure
sound doctrine" (Matt. 24:12, KJV; 2 Tim. 4:3, KJV).

What do I mean by sound doctrine? Sound doctrine is the kind of doctrine that converts men's
hearts.

A Sober Realization for Ministers of God

When you understand this Word, then you know
that at some point you are not going to be the most
popular person. You know that you are going to take
a stand that is going to bring you much persecution—as it has me.

I know who I am called to be for God. I know the
kind of prophet He has called me to be. Some prophets
are called to prophesy "good." Some prophets are

called to prophesy prosperity. But I am called to stand on the wall. I am called to cry loud and spare not. I am called to make God's people aware that while they are getting a new house, a new car and a new job, they need to be trying to get a new heart. The new heart causes us to see the things of God.

The new heart brings the understanding that when everything looks chaotic, because your heart is pure you can see above the chaos and the attacks that Satan blows in your direction. Although you are glancing at the debris surrounding the place where you stand, you can still see God. When you have a pure heart, God is not hidden.

The new heart causes us to see the things of God.

The Lord began to speak to me from Matthew 23:23–24:

> Woe to you, scribes and Pharisees, pretenders (hypocrites)! For you give a tenth of your mint and dill and cummin, and have neglected and omitted the weightier (more important) matters of the Law—right and justice and mercy and fidelity. These you ought [particularly] to have done, without neglecting the others. You blind guides, filtering out a gnat and gulping down a camel!

God began to show me that we, my fellow ministers and prophets of this hour, have begun to concentrate on the houses, the cars, the new jobs and the money that is coming. Yet we have failed to focus on what is most important. Due to lack of prayer, our hearts have become insensitive and, thus, impure. We cannot hear the heartbeat of God. We do not understand that God's heart has picked up the pace. In times past, God "tolerated" certain things. Now, the pace has picked up, and things are different.

Why? God said to me, "After I have come to you and forewarned you over and over again…" God help us. His tolerance level is being weighed down, worn thin, because now people are not walking in iniquity because they are ignorant. They are walking in iniquity because they are rebellious. The Bible says that "rebellion is as the sin of witchcraft" (1 Sam. 15:23).

The Lord says that now the "weightier" thing is our need to get a new heart. If we neglect doing this, the Lord would say from Matthew 23:25–28:

> Woe to you, scribes and Pharisees, pretenders (hypocrites)! For you clean the outside of the cup and of the plate, but within they are full of extortion (prey, spoil, plunder) and grasping self-indulgence. You blind Pharisee! First clean the inside of the cup and of the plate, so that the outside may be clean also.
>
> Woe to you, scribes and Pharisees, pretenders (hypocrites)! For you are like tombs that have been whitewashed, which look beautiful on the outside but inside are full of dead men's bones and everything impure. Just so, you also outwardly seem to people to be just and upright but inside you are full of pretense and lawlessness and iniquity.

A Divine Paradigm Shift

God began to say to me, "In this hour I am calling forth my prophets to purify themselves so that they will not prophesy through eyes of deception. Looking at this 'glorious' church and prophesying of her beauty, they have not been able to see on the inside of the church. She is full of lawlessness and iniquity and everything that is impure and unclean."

He told me, "I want you to begin to 'major' in what I am majoring in right now. It is a fact that I am taking My people along a certain route, and I am blessing them. I am allowing them to get the things that their hearts desire, because this will be the catalyst that I will use to prove to them that it was never Me they wanted. They wanted Me for *things*—they wanted Me for a car, they wanted Me for a house, they wanted Me for a job and for a new husband.

"When I give them everything that their heart desires, and when a newfound walk in Me does not come out of that, or a new heart, then I am showing them that they were never after a walk of righteousness when they came to Me." Then He took me to the prayer of Jeremiah:

> O Lord, though our iniquities testify against us
> [prays Jeremiah], deal and work with us for
> Your own sake [that the heathen may witness
> Your might and faithfulness]! For our back-
> slidings are many; we have sinned against You.
> O Hope of Israel, her Savior in time of trouble,
> why should You be like a sojourner in the land
> and like a wayfaring man who turns aside and
> spreads his tent to tarry [only] for a night? Why

should you be [hesitant and inactive] like a
man stunned and confused, like a mighty man
who cannot save? Yet You, O Lord, are in the
midst of us, and we are called by Your name; do
not leave us!

—JEREMIAH 14:7–9

Hear God's reply beginning in verse 10:

[And the Lord replied to Jeremiah] Thus says
the Lord to His people [Judah]: In the manner
and to the degree already pointed out have they
loved to wander…"

As I read this, He told me, "Though prophets are
crying out to Me on behalf of the people, I have to
allow you, Juanita, to begin to see the nature of the
people." We must be careful that we are not crying
out for a people, or for individuals, who do not even
want God! He said to Jeremiah, "These people are
wanderers…"

God said to Jeremiah, "'To the degree already
pointed out' to you, My people have loved to wander.
They have loved to stray away from Me."

They have not restrained their feet. Therefore
the Lord does not accept them; He will now
[seriously] remember their iniquity and punish
them for their sins. The Lord said to me, Do not
pray for this people for their good. Though they
fast, I will not hear their cry; and though they
offer burnt offering and cereal offering [without
heartfelt surrender to Me…]

—JEREMIAH 14:11–12

There goes that phrase again, "…without heartfelt surrender…" Even though we are doing many

wonderful things in the body of Christ, God said to me, "Though, Juanita, you are going forth and doing this, and doing that, and fasting...it is not a heartfelt surrender to Me. I still do not see in you that your will has been yielded to Me to the point that you want a new heart."

Then God continued speaking to me from Jeremiah 14:12–13:

> ...or by offering it too late], I will not accept them. But I will consume them by the sword, by famine, and by pestilence. Then said I, Alas, Lord God! Behold, the [false] prophets say to them, You will not see the sword, nor will you have famine, but I [the Lord] will give you an assured peace (peace that lasts, the peace of truth) in this place.

God is sending us a warning. We must be careful that while we are prophesying prosperity and peace, God is not moving in a whole different vein!

> Then the Lord said to me, The [false] prophets prophesy lies in My name. I sent them not, neither have I commanded them, nor have I spoken to them. They prophesy to you a false or pretended vision, a worthless divination [conjuring or practicing magic, trying to call forth the responses supposed to be given by idols], and the deceit of their own minds. Therefore thus says the Lord concerning the [false] prophets who prophesy in My name—although I did not send them—and who say, Sword and famine shall not be in this land: By sword and famine shall those prophets be consumed.
>
> —JEREMIAH 14:14–15

The Lord began to deal with me and say, "If you are going to walk in this office in this last hour, I am compelling you to cry out to My people. Provoke them to desire a new heart. Though you hear one prophet over here..." (I am not saying that God told me these would be false prophets) "...though you hear one prophet over there saying, 'Blessings,' and another saying, 'Peace,' you had better cry out what I am calling YOU to cry out.

"At this time, as I am calling you to cry out concerning the new heart, there is already a remnant of people that I have prepared, and I have already begun to turn their minds. I have set them in the birth canal to receive this conversion. If you dare not speak what I call you to speak, you will cause a host of men and women to be lost in trespasses and sin because you went with the popular prophecy."

I have been asked on many occasions, "Why do you think God is saying this right now? When you look at it, our churches are bigger now than ever before." Yes, but are the people really being delivered? Are they coming into an understanding of the true plan of salvation? Are they coming into an understanding of "counsel," or are they coming into a true understanding of conversion?

I picked up Jeremiah's burden from what he saw, according to his words in chapter 9:

> Oh, that my head were waters and my eyes a reservoir of tears, that I might weep day and night for the slain of the daughter of My people! Oh, that I had in the wilderness a lodging place (a mere shelter) for wayfaring men, that I might leave my people and go away from

> them! For they are all adulterers [rendering
> worship to idols instead of the Lord...]
> —Jeremiah 9:1–2

People are rendering more worship to their pastors, to the beauty of their churches, to the worship
songs than to God, "Who has espoused the people to
Himself" (v. 2). Idols have espoused the people to
themselves!

> They are a gang of treacherous men [faithless
> even to each other]. And they bend their
> tongue, [which is] their bow for the lies [they
> shoot]. And not according to faithfulness do
> they rule and become strong in the land; for
> they proceed from evil to evil, and they do not
> know and understand and acknowledge Me,
> says the Lord. Let everyone beware of his neigh-
> bor and put no trust in any brother. For every
> brother is an utter and complete supplanter
> (one who takes by the heel and trips up, a
> deceiver, a Jacob), and every neighbor goes
> about as a slanderer.
> —Jeremiah 9:2–4

Do you still want to know why we need a new
heart? Verses 5 and 6 say:

> And they deceive and mock everyone his neigh-
> bor and do not speak the truth. They have
> taught their tongues to speak lies; they weary
> themselves committing iniquity. Your habita-
> tion is in the midst of deceit [oppression upon
> oppression and deceit upon deceit]; through
> deceit they refuse to know and understand Me,
> says the Lord.

What did God say about the heart in Jeremiah 17? He said that above all things, the heart is desperately wicked and deceitful. When you see that wickedness and deceit are prevalent in our churches and in our society, then you know that *the church must seek God for the new heart.*

> Therefore thus says the Lord of hosts: Behold, I will melt them [by the process of affliction to remove the dross] and test them, for how else should I deal with the daughter of My people? Their tongue is a murderous arrow; it speaks deceitfully; one speaks peaceably to his neighbor with his mouth, but in his heart he lays snares and waits in ambush for him.
>   —JEREMIAH 9:7–8

I want to repeat this: "Their tongue is a murderous arrow; it speaks deceitfully; one speaks peaceably to his neighbor with his mouth, but in his heart he lays snares and waits in ambush for him." God help us.

This verse indicates that there is a match, a parallel, between Israel in Jeremiah's day and the church in this final hour. For many people, what we say and what we do are two different things. Yet we try to hide who we are and what we do by covering it up with what we say. Eventually that will turn. Why? Because when this wicked heart becomes full and active, having been fed by iniquity, and allows the mind to assume full control, we will see the depths of this old heart operating to its fullest potential.

We will still try to cover it up over and over again saying, "I am not like that." Eventually, though, we will have to face the fact that we have become like the Pharisees in Matthew 12:34, whom Jesus confronted by saying:

> You offspring of vipers! How can you speak good things when you are evil (wicked)? For out of the fullness (the overflow, the super-abundance) of the heart the mouth speaks.

We Cannot Hide From the Truth

You cannot hide who you really are. Eventually, that "old heart" within you will go into full operation. You cannot suppress it. You cannot keep that evil heart from operating. Its nature is to pump. Its nature is to function (operate), and when it begins to operate to its fullest potential, then the words of your mouth are going to speak from the abundance of what is in your heart.

> **If you want to know what you are full of, and what your heart is full of, listen to your conversation.**

Lies, deception and trickery will come out of your mouth. Snares for your brother will escape your lips. Out of your mouth will come greed and lust for the flesh and for things—rather than words reflecting a righteous desire to seek and obey God. If you want to know what you are full of, and what your heart is full of, listen to your conversation.

Everything is naked before Him to whom we must

give an account. (See Hebrews 4:13.) God is calling us today—as leaders—to get *real* and set the pace for others. We must pursue the new heart, or we will not be able to understand and obey what He is telling us to do.

Chapter 4

The Prophetic
Word Deepens

The Lord continued to forewarn me as He led me to Ezekiel 13. As He spoke to me, I realized that not only did I not want to bring the Word to others, but I also did not want to admit publicly that God had been dealing with me about receiving a new heart. This is the deception.

> Pride goeth before destruction, and an haughty spirit before a fall.
> —Proverbs 16:18, KJV

I recognized the spirit of pride in my thoughts: *You do not want to say that because you preach the gospel; you do not want to tell people that. When pride comes upon you in this way, the tendency is always to cover up. God has started to reveal to me that covering up is not always the best way to help people.* God has shown me (as mentioned in the previous chapter) that conducting our lives so as to look like "The Untouchables"—looking like we have it all together, like we are perfect—does not leave a straight path for others to follow.

The best route for people to travel is to follow a path that has already been trodden. This is the point of true leadership, the heritage of spiritual fathers and mothers. Since we have already walked the spiritual road that others travel, just like a mother or father in the natural realm, we should be willing to share these experiences with our "children" so that they (and their children) can learn by the same pattern and example.

God explained to me, "I am trying to show you that when you get a new heart, you may be tempted from without, but there is no sin from within. That which is coming 'from without' will not find a match or an identification with anything that is 'within' you. You will be able to stand in times of testing. You will be able to stand against temptation. You will be able to stand against the wiles of Satan."

Then He took me to Ezekiel 13, helping me to understand that as a prophet in this hour, I could no longer keep my mouth shut. I could no longer silence the heartbeat of God.

> And the word of the Lord came to me, saying, Son of man, prophesy against the prophets of Israel who prophesy, and say to those who prophesy out of their own mind and heart, Hear the word of the Lord! Thus says the Lord God: Woe to the foolish prophets who follow their own spirit [and things they have not seen] and have seen nothing! O Israel, your prophets have been like foxes among ruins and in waste places. You have not gone up into the gaps or breaches...
>
> —EZEKIEL 13:1–5

In other words, God was saying, "You have not fortified the walls of My people, you have not 'deposited' in them to the degree that their inner man has been strengthened against the onslaught of Satan." Because His prophets have not done this, today we watch as many believers are "taken out" and slaughtered in the battle of the Lord!

Why did Jesus have His disciples with Him at all times? What was the requirement?

What is this battle? The apostle Paul described the battle when he said, "For the desires of the flesh are opposed to the [Holy] Spirit, and the [desires of the] Spirit are opposed to the flesh (godless human nature)" (Gal. 5:17). If walls have not been built up according to Ezekiel 13:5...if no one is standing in the gap...if no one has grabbed the horns of the altar ...if no one has lamented and demonstrated the "pattern" of lament...if no one has shown the saints how to walk, suffer and endure...then there is no example to show people know how to stand during the battle of the Lord.

Have you ever wondered, "Why did Jesus have His disciples walk with Him at all times? What was the requirement?"

It was necessary for the disciples to learn how to follow the steps of Jesus, just as it had been necessary for Jesus to learn how to follow the steps of His Father. They needed to observe Jesus walking in the

breaches (paths) of the Father in order to be taught
how to operate in signs, wonders and miracles. He
had to show them the *pattern* for going through the
breaches that He had learned through obedience to
His own Father. The disciples learned how to submit
by watching Jesus' example. He taught them, by
example, how to be persecuted without warring
back. He showed them how to be whipped with cat-
o'-nine-tails and never say a mumbling word. He
showed them how to suffer for righteousness' sake.

- He showed them how to go to the cross
  and die for the sins of the world.

- He demonstrated how to sacrifice and
  lay down their lives for a brother.

- He showed them how to "stand in the
  gap" for someone that needed God.

Jesus lived a pattern. As a result, when Peter was
persecuted, he knew how to die. Paul knew how to
die. The disciples and early followers of Jesus had all
been taught how to die. They understood the pattern
and knew how to stand in the battle of the Lord.

Prophets Who Prophesy False Hope

> They have seen falsehood and lying divination,
> saying, The Lord says; but the Lord has not
> sent them. Yet they have hoped and made men
> to hope for the confirmation of their word.
>
> —EZEKIEL 13:6

The prophets who prophesied false hopes to the
people caused men to believe that the "peace" about

which they were prophesying was possible. They gave the impression that God was "understanding" of the spiritual lethargy present among His people.

Just as in the days of Ezekiel, people everywhere are trusting in the voice of the prophet who comes in God's stead. They are looking for a confirmation of what the prophet has spoken. But in reality, what the prophet has spoken is not what God is saying. Many people have become gripped by false hope, which will bring them into despair and land them in a final state of hopelessness. When hopelessness penetrates their trust in God, they will fall by the wayside.

The Word of the Lord continues in verses 7–11:

> Have you not seen a false vision and have you not spoken a lying divination when you say, The Lord says, although I have not spoken? Therefore thus says the Lord God: Because you have spoken empty, false, and delusive words and have seen lies, therefore behold, I am against you, says the Lord God. And My hand shall be against the prophets who see empty, false, and delusive visions and who give lying prophecies. They shall not be in the secret counsel of My people, nor shall they be recorded in the register of the house of Israel, nor shall they enter into the land of Israel; and you shall know (understand and realize) that I am the Lord God. Because, even because they have seduced My people, saying, Peace, when there is no peace, and because when one builds a [flimsy] wall, behold, [these prophets] daub it over with whitewash, say to them who daub it with whitewash that it shall fall!

Once again, God is warning against taking on the cloak of the outward appearance. Many are deceived into indulging in the seduction of glamour that Christendom brings. Yet God's prophets, His watchmen, do not speak the truth to these people about their need to go deeper in God.

When we stand back and watch people build flimsy walls on things that have no substance, and then turn around and daub them with whitewash, we are saying, "That is good. At least you are not where you used to be…that is wonderful. You are doing fine."

God is saying that if I refuse to preach this new heart message…if I refuse to give you truth to help you understand that we all need a new heart, then I am setting you up for a fall, because that flimsy wall in Christendom shall fall.

> There shall be a downpour of rain; and you, O great hailstones, shall fall, and a violent wind shall tear apart [the whitewashed, flimsy wall].
> —EZEKIEL 13:11

When the enemy comes in and when the storms of life are blowing, many fall by the wayside. They had only the outward appearance of a flimsy wall that had been whitewashed by a false prophet. They have no depth in God because they have not yet received the new heart.

Ezekiel 13:12 continues:

> Behold, when the wall is fallen, will you not be asked, Where is the coating with which you [prophets] daubed it?

When people fall into error and cannot find their

way out...when they are launched into an era of darkness, then are you certain that you will not be approached again by these same people, who will say, "You are a man or a woman of God. I thought you said that 'this' or 'that' was all right. I thought you said that nothing was wrong with this. I thought you said that God understood. Why am I in the situation that I am in right now? Why am I being attacked the way that I am being attacked now?"

As men and women of God...as God's spokesmen in this dark world, we must be certain that we have not prophesied false hope to a spiritually lethargic people.

You Cannot Lead People Farther Than You Have Gone

God revealed to me that when He has set you into a position, but you do not have depth in Him, you can only preach from the realm in which you walk. You can only raise a person up to the level on which you stand. The depth of your deliverance is the depth of deliverance you can offer to another. There has to be purification in the priesthood, purification in leadership.

Leaders must begin to seek God for the new heart, so that, by way of example, they can provoke the people to want the new heart.

> Therefore thus says the Lord God: I will even rend it with a stormy wind in My wrath, and there shall be an overwhelming rain in My

anger and great hailstones in wrath to destroy
[that wall].

—EZEKIEL 13:13

God is saying, "You think that you are secure and
that you have it all together. But I am telling you that
if you have no depth in Me, and if you do not receive
this new heart..."

There has to be purification in the priesthood, purification in leadership.

The Word of the Lord is coming to you to say, "I
am going to send a wind, and that wind is going to
blow. I am going to release the hailstones to come in
an awesome, overwhelming rain. I am doing this
because I love you. I am doing this to break down
the wall so that you can see you are not as strong as
you think you are. You do not need structure only—
you need a deposit. You need to be transformed. You
need to be converted.

"When I look and see those that I have chosen
before the foundation of the world to be born again
and transformed, and I see a false prophet trying to
help them construct something that is not going to
be able to stand, then I have no other choice but to
send a wind to blow it down. That wind will keep
blowing it down. It will keep you in the fiery fur-
nace...in the realm of affliction...to show you that
there is another depth, another height, to which I

am calling you." *Thus says the Lord!*

In Ezekiel 13:14, God said:

> So will I break down the wall that you have daubed with whitewash and bring it down to the ground, so that its foundations will be exposed; when it falls, you will perish and be consumed in the midst of it. And you will know (understand and realize) that I am the Lord.

God is reiterating, "You will know, you will understand and realize that it was not Me, that it was not of God, because that which is of God is eternal. That which is of God stands the test of time. That which is of God has already been tried in the fire and has come out as pure gold."

> Thus will I accomplish My wrath upon the wall and upon those who have daubed it with whitewash, and I will say to you, The wall is no more, neither are they who daubed it, the [false] prophets of Israel who prophesied deceitfully about Jerusalem, seeing visions of peace for her when there is no peace, says the Lord God. And you, son of man, set your face against the daughters of your people who prophesy out of [the wishful thinking of] their own minds and hearts; prophesy against them, and say, Thus says the Lord God: Woe to the women who sew pillows to all armholes and fasten magic, protective charms to all wrists, and deceptive veils upon the heads of those of every stature to hunt and capture human lives! Will you snare the lives of My people to keep your own selves alive?
>
> —EZEKIEL 13:15–18

In this last hour we are being confronted with an order of priesthood that chooses to ensnare people's lives by prophesying and preaching lies—by not giving them the Word of the Lord according to the meat of the Word—in order to keep *themselves* alive.

God Led Me Into a Death Walk

When God began to say, "I want you to preach the new heart," then there had to be a death realm for me. There had to be an "exposing" for me. I had to come to the realization "publicly" that I needed a new heart and that there were things going on inside of me that did not please God.

If you come to the place where you say, "I am called of God to prophesy," "I am called of God to be a teacher," or "I am called of God to preach the gospel to the poor and to open blind eyes and set the captives free," then at some point, you will be compelled to give up your own life, even your reputation if necessary, to save the lives of God's people. If you hold on to your own life, walking around as if you have never done anything wrong, as if everything in your life is perfect, you will set a snare and hang a veil that will blind people to the truth. If people are veiled, they cannot see God. If their hearts are snared, they will surely die. Ezekiel 13:19 reads:

> You have profaned Me among My people [in payment] for handfuls of barley and for pieces of bread, slaying persons who should not die and giving [a guaranty of] life to those who

should not live, by your lying to My people, who give heed to lies.

In other words, "Because you cannot get to the point..." He said to me, "Because people are bringing you offerings and giving you gifts, and because they are willing to do this for you..." God did not have to say any more.

Think about it. We are part of a priesthood that drives the best cars and wears the finest suits, alligator shoes and St. John knits—and we are giving "peace" to people whom God has already cursed and who should die. And we are telling people who should live that they are going to die!

If people are veiled, they cannot see God. If their hearts are snared, they will surely die.

We have the gospel backward. We say to those who are compromising and living close to the edge of the world, "You are wonderful; you are going to be all right." Yet they have no desire to "sell out" to God.

But to people who are dying to the flesh and giving up all to follow God, we tell them—through a false revelation and evaluation of their circumstance— "You are going too deep." "You pray too much." "You are a little too righteous." "You are going a little too far off the deep end." "Be careful; you'll drive yourself crazy by praying every day for two or three hours."

We are pronouncing death to people who are selling

out to God, and we are pronouncing life to people who walk in carnality according to the spirit of this world. We are blinded by our own deception. We are blinded by the "old heart." Ezekiel 13:20 continues:

> Therefore thus says the Lord God: Behold, I am against your pillows and charms and veils with which you snare human lives like birds, and I will tear them from your arms and will let the lives you hunt go free, the lives you are snaring like birds.

We are blinded by our own deception. We are blinded by the "old heart."

"You may think you are getting away with it," God is saying, "but it's *only for a season!*"

Hear the Word of the Lord as it comes across this page into the heart of every preacher and teacher: "If you do not begin to teach the full gospel…if you do not begin to warn My people about their ways and provoke them to make sure that they have the heart that is pure…then I am going to snare them from you, and I am going to cause those that have been snared by you to go free. You yourself will be destroyed."

> Your [deceptive] veils also will I tear and deliver My people out of your hand…Then you shall know (understand and realize) that I am the Lord.
>
> —Ezekiel 13:21

God's people will no longer remain in the hands of those who do not lead them to the new heart. If you have failed to deliver God's people, your ministry will fall. If I have failed, my ministry shall surely fall.

> Because with lies you have made the righteous sad and disheartened, whom I have not made sad or disheartened, and because you have encouraged and strengthened the hands of the wicked, that he should not return from his wicked way and be saved [in that you falsely promised him life], therefore you will no more see false visions or practice divinations, and I will deliver My people out of your hand. Then you will know (understand and realize) that I am the Lord.
>
> —EZEKIEL 13:22–23

The Time for Change Has Come

Trust me when I tell you that we have not seen the falling away. We have not seen the judgment of God as we will see it one day. God is speaking to leadership in this chapter, calling us to fulfill our destiny in ministry by provoking His people to walk in the Spirit so they do not give heed to the things of the flesh. We must redirect this walk of faith to a "heart" thing, not a "flesh" thing...a righteous experience, not a worldly one.

As pastors, teachers or prophets in this hour of preaching the gospel, we should be feeling the temperature of the Spirit realm. We must cry out to the hearts of God's people, according to Hebrews 3:12–13, and say:

[Therefore beware] brethren, take care, lest there be in any one of you a wicked, unbelieving heart [which refuses to cleave to, trust in, and rely on Him], leading you to turn away and desert or stand aloof from the living God. But instead warn (admonish, urge, and encourage) one another every day, as long as it is called Today, that none of you may be hardened [into settled rebellion] by the deceitfulness of sin [by the fraudulence, the stratagem, the trickery which the delusive glamour of his sin may play on him].

We are living in the final hour, and the glamour of the world is causing us to be tricked by the enemy. The "outer cloak" is deceiving us. The Word of the Lord is constantly ringing in my spirit that we have the "form of godliness," but we are "denying the power thereof" (2 Tim. 3:5, KJV). We have everything that it takes to make up the "image" of God, but the *real power* is being able to say *yes* to God and *no* to the devil.

Even while you are reading these words, as a prophet of God I bind the hand of the enemy that would try to come upon you with fear to keep you from making a righteous stand.

Preach the New Heart Message

Now just as Jannes and Jambres were hostile to and resisted Moses, so these men also are hostile to and oppose the Truth. They have depraved and distorted minds, and are reprobate and counterfeit and to be rejected as far as the faith is concerned. But they will not get very

far, for their rash folly will become obvious to
everybody, as was that of those [magicians men-
tioned]. Now you have closely observed and diligently followed my teaching, conduct, purpose
in life, faith, patience, love, steadfastness...

—2 TIMOTHY 3:8–10

Timothy is describing a person who has received
the new heart. This is the only kind of person who
can preach this message. You cannot preach dili-
gence, conduct, purpose in life, faith, patience, love
and steadfastness unless you have first received
these characteristics from God. I encourage you to
keep reading, and you will discover the truth that I
found about this "new heart." This revelation literally shocked me into silence as I sat in awe of God,
pondering the depths of His handiwork.

What comes from the heart goes to the heart, as
we read in Psalm 42:7: "Deep calleth to the deep"
(KJV).

We have everything that
it takes to make up the
"image" of God, but the
real power is being
able to say *yes* to God
and *no* to the devil.

In the third chapter of 2 Timothy we read: "Now
you have closely observed and diligently followed my
teaching, conduct, purpose in life, faith, patience,
love, steadfastness..." Watch out; it is getting ready
to go deeper: "...persecutions, sufferings—such as

occurred to me at Antioch, at Iconium, and at Lystra, persecutions I endured, but out of them all the Lord delivered me" (2 Tim. 3:10–11).

That's right. As you stand and provoke people to go after the new heart, you will be persecuted. God, however, has promised in His Word that He will deliver you out of every one.

> Indeed all who delight in piety and are determined to live a devoted and godly life in Christ Jesus will meet with persecution [will be made to suffer because of their religious stand]. But wicked men and imposters will go on from bad to worse, deceiving and leading astray others and being deceived and led astray themselves. But as for you, continue to hold to the things that you have learned and of which you are convinced, knowing from whom you learned [them], and how from your childhood you have had a knowledge of and been acquainted with the sacred Writings, which are able to instruct you and give you the understanding for salvation which comes through faith in Christ Jesus [through the leaning of the entire human personality on God in Christ Jesus in absolute trust and confidence in His power, wisdom, and goodness].
>
> Every scripture is God-breathed (given by His inspiration) and profitable for instruction, for reproof and conviction of sin…
>
> —2 TIMOTHY 3:12–16

The Scriptures were not written to make people jump and shout, or to make them believe things like: "Oh, I am going to get a car." "I am going to get a house." "My life is going to be perfect when I get saved." No! The power that is coming—and this new level of the Word that is about to hit this twenty-first century—is going to be the kind of gospel that will help you to determine who has been in the prayer closet with God, who has received a new heart and who knows the heartbeat of God. The gospel that they will preach will be according to 2 Timothy!

It will be "profitable for instruction, for reproof and conviction of sin…" Watch out! It is not for acquiring houses and cars. It is not for acquiring prosperity, although prosperity is a part of righteous living. It is true that when you "seek ye first the kingdom of God, and his righteousness…all these things shall be added" (Matt. 6:33, KJV). Absolutely! The balance of that Word, and the balance of the power of that message, is the fact that GOD "breathed" it!

Scripture says, "Every scripture is God-breathed (given by His inspiration) and profitable for instruction, for reproof and conviction of sin." Though God inspired the writing of all Scripture, there are seasons when He "breathes" on a certain text. There are times and seasons in our world when God "breathes" on a certain Word in order to get a certain assignment done for a certain season and era. He does this because He knows what is up the road.

If we are preaching a gospel in this hour that is not a God-breathed Word for this season, there will be no conviction of sin even though we slap our hips, turn up the organ and get people to shout back at us. Without that conviction of sin, we are merely covering them up with sheets while they speak in tongues, run around the church or fall to their knees.

When God took me down through this passage, I had no other choice but to hear the Word of the

Lord. I even wrote a little footnote on the side of this
scripture that said *yes* to God. When He said, "Read
on, daughter," and I did, He declared, "Now I charge
you…"

There are times and seasons in our world when God "breathes" on a certain Word in order to get a certain assignment done for a certain season and era.

Just as He charged me with that truth, I charge
you today, reader. If you have this book in your
hand, God is redirecting *your* spirit! Second
Timothy 4:1–2 says:

> I charge [you] in the presence of God and of
> Christ Jesus, Who is to judge the living and the
> dead, and by (in the light of) His coming and His
> kingdom; herald and preach the Word! Keep
> your sense of urgency [stand by, be at hand and
> ready], whether the opportunity seems to be
> favorable or unfavorable. [Whether it is conven-
> ient or inconvenient, whether it is welcome or
> unwelcome, you as preacher of the Word are to
> show people in what way their lives are wrong].

This is my assignment—not to encourage people
in doing wrong, but to show God's people where
their lives are *wrong*. And to:

> Convince them, rebuking and correcting, warn-
> ing and urging and encouraging them, being
> unflagging and inexhaustible in patience and
> teaching. For the time is coming when [people]
> will not tolerate (endure) sound and wholesome
> instruction, but, having ears itching [for some-
> thing pleasing and gratifying], they will gather to
> themselves one teacher after another to a con-
> siderable number, chosen to satisfy their own
> liking and to foster the errors they hold.
>
> —2 TIMOTHY 4:2–3

It is our charge to teach people how to take responsibility for their errors. People should not say, "The
reason I am this way is because Pastor So-and-so told
me that it was all right," or "The reason I operate the
way I do is because Pastor So-and-so told me that God
understood."

It is also our charge—first and foremost—to say
and do exactly what God commands. We are not to
preach what we *think* the people need or want to
hear. We are to preach and teach at God's direction,
and let Him take care of the rest. In 2 Peter 2:15–19,
the Lord said:

> Forsaking the straight road they have gone
> astray; they have followed the way of Balaam
> [the son] of Beor, who loved the reward of
> wickedness. But he was rebuked for his own
> transgression when a dumb beast of burden
> spoke with human voice and checked the
> prophet's madness. These are springs without
> water and mists driven along before a tempest,
> for whom is reserved forever the gloom of dark-
> ness. For uttering loud boasts of folly, they
> beguile and lure with lustful desires of the flesh
> those who are barely escaping from them who

are wrongdoers. They promise them liberty,
when they themselves are the slaves of deprav-
ity and defilement—for by whatever anyone is
made inferior or worse or is overcome, to that
[person or thing] he is enslaved.

We cannot allow ourselves to be enslaved to
deception, especially while we are doing God's work!
We must serve God from a new heart, one that only
He can give and that we must maintain. He is charg-
ing us to turn it around, to set our faces like "flints"
toward His divine purpose in this final hour. Second
Timothy 4:4–5 concludes our charge:

> ...and will turn aside from hearing the truth
> and wander off into myths and man-made fic-
> tions. As for you, be calm and cool and steady,
> accept and suffer unflinchingly every hardship,
> do the work of an evangelist, fully perform all
> the duties of your ministry.

Chapter 5

The Heart: **Who Can Know It?**

Yes, we have a problem, and ministers of God bear a great responsibility. This, however, does not abort the individual's responsibility to pursue the new heart. Each one of us will be required to give an account to God for our words and actions (Matt. 12:36; Heb. 4:13). We have all been infected with a diseased, old heart, which is trying to rule us. How can we "know" this deceived heart?

I have already touched on certain aspects of the old heart. In order for you to understand fully God's message in this hour, I must continue to build the case that the old heart does exist. It is important to understand that there are people in the world—and in the church—who have the old heart. We all need the new heart.

Jeremiah 17 is the foundation for what God is saying. He is trying to get—and keep—our attention. It is vital that we understand this truth. The very first thing we discover about the heart in Jeremiah 17:9 is that it is "deceitful above all things."

When the Lord first began revealing this Word to

me, I did not want to hear it. I had already seen the signs of my own shortcomings, but I felt they were just part of my character. In reality, I was taking the easy way out.

The Grace Factor

Many times believers abuse the fact that there is a "grace factor" in our walk with God. We assume a comfortable position where we do not have to change certain behaviors because we know that grace is there. Through our own spiritual laziness, we are using the liberty of Christ as an occasion for the flesh.

> What shall we say [to all this]? Are we to remain in sin in order that God's grace (favor and mercy) may multiply and overflow? Certainly not! How can we who died to sin live in it any longer? Are you ignorant of the fact that all of us who have been baptized into Christ Jesus were baptized into His death? We were buried therefore with Him by the baptism into death, so that just as Christ was raised from the dead by the glorious [power] of the Father, so we too might [habitually] live and behave in the newness of life.
>
> —Romans 6:1–4

After God birthed this truth into my spirit, I began recognizing personality traits manifesting from within me that were evidence of the old heart. Each time this happened, I would simply say, "Lord, forgive me." But after a period of time, they would resurface—sometimes on a daily basis! Even though

I repented each time, they would come to the surface again.

I know that God was giving me *opportunities* to allow my mind to be transformed. But, like many other people, rather than spending quality time to find out why these shortcomings kept surfacing and trying to understand why I kept failing in those areas, *for the sake of comfort* I attached those things to myself and said, "This is just a part of my personality." "This is just the way I am." "God understands the way I am." I had made myself comfortable, and I settled into this lethargic frame of mind.

When you fall into this trap, it extends to your inner circle and to your immediate surroundings. Then the deception worsens. Rather than you having to adjust and change some things about your personality and character, your friends and associates begin to accept that behavior as just being "you" because it has become such a part of you. They reposition their personalities and characters to adjust or make room for that part of you, which has not been purified.

As a result, you stay the way you are. Once people become accustomed to your "old heart" behavior, they avoid it. Everybody makes sure they do not do anything to bring that part of your temperament to the surface. If it surfaces, they say, "Well, that is just the way she is."

And you do the same thing about their "old heart" behavior. You end up saying the same thing about them. We forget that the Bible has told us not to know anyone "after the flesh" (2 Cor. 5:16, KJV).

The Lord began to make me understand that He

was not requiring me to *adjust* these shortcomings for *acceptance sake*—He was requiring me to *change*.

Self-Deception

The first thing God had to break was my deception about myself, because "the heart is deceitful above all things" (Jer. 17:9). My own heart was deceiving me. That got me! After being raised in the church and being saved, I constantly "fell away," doing things that were outside of God's will. I came to this realization—your heart can be deceived without your knowing it, because you live for God from the "religious factor."

What do I mean by a *religious factor*? It's when we compare our righteousness to the righteousness of other people, rather than to God's. We measure who we are as compared to another person. You will always find someone who you "feel" is worse off, or "less all right," than you. Evaluating yourself by comparing against others (who are equally as imperfect as you are) is a subtle trick of the enemy.

When you compare yourself with someone else, your heart deceives you into thinking, *I am not all that bad. Look at how bad So-and-so is.* Or you could compare yourself with someone and think, *Well, he and I, or she and I, are a lot alike, so I am not all that bad.*

You begin to identify with the behavior of others, attempting to mimic "the going personality" in Christendom at the time. Everybody does the same thing—that which is *familiar* and *acceptable*. We are all stuck in a bucket like a bunch of crabs, saying, "This is the 'Christian' way, and everybody is like this." Everyone settles in and gets comfortable with that particular lifestyle until the Lord reveals to someone that there is more. There is much more to following Him than stumbling and blundering around with the crowd.

> # Your heart can be deceived without your knowing it, because you live for God from the "religious factor."

The sad thing is that your mind will do anything to protect itself—even conflicting things. For example, it pushes blame toward some while at the same time identifying with others, all to justify itself. The reason for this is the fact that everything entering the brain is first processed through our emotions. Our emotions, like it or not, decide what is or is not *relevant* before logic sorts things out. This is the danger of the old heart.

Only the new heart can see through this. If you ask God for the new heart, you can begin to pursue the perfection of God and walk out what you believe to the extent that your heart becomes "perfected" in Him.

When this happens, you will stop comparing yourself to others. You will allow God to evaluate you properly. He can inspect your heart and give you the right grade. If He gives your heart an F, then you know it is failing, as mine was. But God will give you a new heart!

Unsaved or Fallen Away?

Revelation 2:4–5 (KJV) warns:

> Nevertheless I have somewhat against thee, because thou hast left thy first love. Remember therefore from whence thou art fallen, and repent, and do the first works; or else I will come unto thee quickly, and will remove thy candlestick out of his place, except thou repent.

How do you know when you need a new heart? How do you know the difference between making a mistake and falling away from your first love?

A Step-by-Step Process

Ephesians 4 gives us a step-by-step process to teach us to recognize when we have fallen away from our first love and need a new heart.

> So this I say and solemnly testify [in the name of] the Lord [as in His presence], that you must no longer live as the heathen (the Gentiles) do in their perverseness [in the folly, vanity, and emptiness of their souls and the futility] of their minds.
>
> —Ephesians 4:17

1. A "futile" mind is incapable of producing any result.

Remember that a "futile" mind is incapable of producing any result; it is ineffective, useless and unsuccessful. The thought patterns of this mind do not yield anything that is fruitful or beneficial. This first step is when we look at things our own way and pervert the Word of God.

2. Our moral understanding is darkened.

"Their moral understanding is darkened and their reasoning is beclouded" (v. 18). This is the second step. When you start doing ungodly things and yet try to justify why you are doing it, your moral understanding is darkened, and your reasoning is beclouded.

3. We explain away our actions according to worldly knowledge and carnal information.

"[They are] alienated (estranged, self-banished) from the life of God [with no share in it: this is] because of the ignorance (the want of knowledge and perception...)" (v. 18). We are living in a brain world. This world moves according to knowledge, not according to the new heart. It is propelled by our mind and the lust for knowledge, which brings personal power. Everybody is in a sweat to gain more information and knowledge. Yet they are still ignorant about God and His ways; they are like the people described in 2 Timothy 3:7, who "...are never able to arrive at a recognition and knowledge of the Truth."

As a result, we try to cover our actions by "explaining them away" according to worldly knowledge and carnal information. Gaining this knowledge and information can, once again, deceive the old heart into thinking, *I am filled with great knowledge; therefore, I have an understanding of God.* Not so. You may read the Bible and comprehend it according to the English language, but the only way that you can understand it according to the Spirit is by virtue of the new heart.

4. We persistently do things our own way.

Ephesians 4:18 continues, "(...the willful blindness) that is deep-seated in them, due to their hardness of heart [to the insensitiveness of their moral nature]." This is step 4—persistently doing things our way. We have become *willfully* blinded, not *incapable* of seeing. We have chosen it. That is why this verse says the blindness is "deep-seated." We have been doing something a certain way for years and years, until we finally *believe* that we are walking in God's ways when in fact we are in error. Our hearts have become hardened and insensitive to what is right before God.

> In their spiritual apathy they have become callous and past feeling and reckless and have abandoned themselves [a prey] to unbridled sensuality, eager and greedy to indulge in every form of impurity [that their depraved desires may suggest and demand]. But you did not so learn Christ!
>
> —Ephesians 4:19–20

This is saying that from all of the understanding and knowledge that you have gained, these "sensual" things continue to manifest in your life on a daily basis. I am not talking about when you make a mistake every now and then. You do these things on a daily basis—to the point that you have become "willfully blind." Your heart has been hardened, and you have become insensitive to the fact that you are living a reckless life before God.

5. You indulge in every impurity that comes your way.

You may have learned the vocabulary of Scripture, but you have not learned Christ. You have not spiritually comprehended the purpose and reason why He died. Therefore, as I said in chapter two, you have become prey to the influences of the world and the enemy. Since you have not learned Christ, you indulge in every impurity that comes your way. This is the fifth, and final, step. Verses 21–24 say:

> Assuming that you have really heard Him and been taught by Him, as [all] Truth is in Jesus [embodied and personified in Him], strip yourselves of your former nature [put off and discard your old unrenewed self] which characterized your previous manner of life and becomes corrupt through lusts and desires that spring from delusion; and be constantly renewed in the spirit of your mind [having a fresh mental and spiritual attitude], and put on the new nature (the regenerate self) created in God's image [Godlike] in true righteousness and holiness.

Do you see a negative pattern forming in your life? If so, you need a new heart.

The Deception of the Flesh

~⌒~⌒~

Before I move on to the works of the flesh, I want to make sure that you understand the fullness of what *flesh* means. It refers either to the physical body or the human nature (as opposed to the nature of God) with its "frailties…and passions." The flesh is you—in the natural—inside and out. The "internal" flesh is part of your old heart and your unrenewed mind, which causes the "external" flesh to disobey God.

> But I say, walk and live [habitually] in the [Holy] Spirit [responsive to and controlled and guided by the Spirit]; then you will certainly not gratify the cravings and desires of the flesh (of human nature without God). For the desires of the flesh are opposed to the [Holy] Spirit, and the [desires of the] Spirit are opposed to the flesh (godless human nature); for these are antagonistic to each other [continually withstanding and in conflict with each other], so that you are not free but are prevented from doing what you desire to do. But if you are guided (led) by the [Holy] Spirit, you are not subject to the Law.
>
> —GALATIANS 5:16–18

Verses 19–21 spell out the works of the flesh— *read closely:*

> Now the doings (practices) of the flesh are clear (obvious): they are immorality, impurity, indecency, idolatry, sorcery, enmity, strife, jealousy, anger (ill temper), selfishness, divisions (dissensions), party spirit (factions, sects with peculiar opinions, heresies), envy,

> drunkenness, carousing, and the like. I warn
> you beforehand, just as I did previously, that
> those who do such things shall not inherit the
> kingdom of God.

These are just *some* of the characteristics of the
heart that are being made manifest. Jeremiah 17:9
said that the heart is desperately wicked; who can
know it? This must mean that we can only name
some of the traits. Attached to these things, and
behind them, are other things that have been
"lodged" in the "old heart," things that have not yet
come to light.

The Deception of "Control"

Have you ever been in a situation where you said to
yourself, "I will never do this" or "I will never do
that"? I cannot tell you how many times I said that
I would never do something, and then ended up
doing just that. This is because the old heart is on a
timetable, to the degree that when it is allowed to
remain within you, it becomes stronger by being fed
the worldly knowledge from the brain. We "house"
this old heart until every evil work from the bottom
of the pit comes to the surface.

Think about it. How can a man walk into a school
and start stabbing small children? Where does it
come from? How can a person get a shotgun, walk
into a McDonald's and just start firing away and killing
people? What do you think gets inside of a terrorist,
causing him to ram a plane into the Twin Towers in
New York City? These people did not simply plan to

do these things. The depths of that evil heart were manifesting.

It starts small, with the things that you "think" you can control—which becomes the next deception of Satan. He allows you to think that you are in control of this "old heart." He allows you to think, *I have it under control. I only drank one drink.* Or, *I only smoked one cigarette.* He knows that if you keep going—keep letting that heart go unchallenged, unchanged and unconverted—everything in that old heart (that he has birthed into the world) will be made manifest in your life.

Who can know this heart? Who would want this heart to remain in them, not knowing the full ability of evil that sits inside of us?

We have become walking time bombs. We have become accidents waiting to happen. We have become "accessible" to anything that Satan desires to do in the earth—a prey for his next assignment. How can you tell him *no* when he is the ruler of that heart? Going back to my friend's comment, it saddens me to think that the enemy's ways seem to be more "attainable" than the gospel—only because we have failed to ask God for a "new heart."

The Spirit of the Lord does not govern the old heart because it does not belong to Him. It is the heart of Satan. So anything that Satan puts forth for us to do, if we have the old heart, we cannot rebuke it. We cannot say, "I refuse to do that," because we are housing his heart.

We must realize this heart is destined for eternal judgment. It has already been prepared, because of what it carries, to go to eternal damnation.

Therefore, it will never lead you to life, because it does not have life in it. It will never lead you to eternal truth, because this heart does not have the ability to house the Word of the Lord.

Transformation takes place when our minds are brought to the understanding that we need God.

I can always tell when an individual is coming to the end of self. Death fights to remain in control as life begins the transformation within—and the struggle comes to the surface. As light emerges, God says:

> You are the light of the world. A city set on a hill cannot be hidden. Nor do men light a lamp and put it under a peck measure, but on a lampstand...Let your light so shine before men that they may see your moral excellence and your praiseworthy, notable, and good deeds and recognize and honor and praise and glorify your Father Who is in heaven.
>
> —MATTHEW 5:14–16

God has put His light within us to shine before the world, not to suppress and hide it from others. He does not want to remove the candlestick "from its place" (Rev. 2:5). He is calling us to repent.

We do not recognize God's mercy in His plan of salvation. What a privilege and an honor it is when He calls us out of sin and gives us the opportunity to become acquainted with Him! This is the biggest miracle that can happen in your life, because—in the midst of having a mind that has been "conceived" in sin and "shaped" in iniquity, trained by the world and the enemy to the point that you have come into the world *prepared* to die an eternal death—God is still able to penetrate it.

God allows us to hear the gospel, and at that very moment, in that split second of time, He penetrates the mind that had been trained by Satan. He puts His Word in our mind, so that it tells us to "...be not conformed to this world: but by ye transformed by the renewing of your mind, that ye may prove what is that good, and acceptable, and perfect, will of God" (Rom. 12:2, KJV).

Transformation takes place when our minds are brought to the understanding that we need God.

The Spiritual Emergency Room

When we do not "renew" our minds, we can "fall away" into the old heart. In my studies, I have learned that the brain never stops working. It never settles down, nor does it ever shut up. Even when you are sleeping, the brain is in motion. The brain (not the heart) constantly races, moves, talks, plans and visualizes. Without stopping for a breath, it takes us to where we have been, where we are and where we are going. It is constantly receiving information at breakneck speed. The majority of the time, the heart cannot, and will not, keep up with the pace of the mind.

I recently had to be taken to the emergency room because I did not understand this principle. You see, many times we are so busy moving and doing things that we do not consider our hearts. I didn't, and I starting experiencing the symptoms. I ended up in the emergency room with chest pains. The doctors started talking to me about heart attacks. As they talked, they explained how defibrillators jump-start a heart that has stopped beating.

This incident reminded me of the church. There are so many Christians racing around with spiritual "heart problems" that we need to be resurrected when we get to church! The choir, the preacher and the praise and worship team have been our spiritual defibrillators—they get powered up and anointed with oil, and they send out an electrical charge into the congregation. They are trying to jump-start hearts that have literally stopped beating. The treatment keeps you going for a couple of days, but that heart is still "mortally sick" (Jer. 17:9). It needs to be replaced.

The Bible says that we were "...dead in trespasses and sins" (Eph. 2:1, KJV). We have living, functioning, breathing hearts that keep our physical bodies alive, but spiritually, we are dead. So we depend on church "mechanics" to bring life. But only a new heart will cause us to live forever.

In the natural realm, when someone has a heart attack, there are signs, sounds and different things that the diseased heart allows to happen in the physical body. There is pain that goes down the arm and down the legs because the arteries are having a hard time pumping blood to and from the heart.

We must also look at the causes for a heart attack. Many times we eat the wrong thing, such as foods that are high in fat and cholesterol. We often do not get proper rest. After my trip to the emergency room, I had to change my diet and quit eating meat and other things that would affect my blood flow. I could not carry the outside weight of my schedule, doing everything that needed to be done, and eat as heavily as I was eating. I had to let something go.

The Spiritual "Vital Signs" of Breakdown

God is saying the same thing in this hour.

> O Jerusalem, wash your heart from wickedness, that ye may be saved! How long shall your iniquitious and grossly offensive thoughts lodge within you? For a voice declares from Dan [in the north] and proclaims evil from Mount Ephraim [the range dividing Israel from Judah].
> —JEREMIAH 4:14–15

In other words, God is saying that if you do not wash your heart, the very thing that you once enjoyed with this old heart will ambush you. Before you know it, the thing that you have built up and enjoy will become your enemy. This passage continues:

> Warn the [neighboring] nations [that our adversary is coming]; announce to Jerusalem that besiegers are coming from a far country, and they shout against the cities of Judah. Like keepers of a field they are against her round

about, because she has been rebellious against Me, says the Lord.

—JEREMIAH 4:16–17

When everything starts folding in and coming against you, God has not done this. Our own rebellion toward God causes our atmosphere to turn. These changes are our *vital signs*, letting us know that it is time to receive a new heart.

> Your ways and your doings have brought these things upon you. This is your calamity and doom; surely it is bitter, for surely it reaches your very heart! [It is not only the prophet but also the people who cry out in their thoughts] My anguish, my anguish! I writhe in pain! Oh, the walls of my heart! My heart is disquieted and throbs aloud within me; I cannot be silent! For I have heard the sound of the trumpet, the alarm of war.
>
> —JEREMIAH 4:18–19

If you do not wash your heart, the very thing that you once enjoyed with this old heart will ambush you.

This is the sound of spiritual vital signs crying out. Our chest cavities cave in because of our own doings! Verse 20 states, "News of one violent disaster and calamity comes close after another."

We cannot turn on the news anymore without hearing about disaster. People are starving; cities are being flooded; fires cannot be put out; there are terrorist attacks. In other countries people are using their own bodies to blow up malls and shopping centers. Children are being raped, and the homeless are going unfed. God help us to discern the "signs" of worldwide heart failure.

The same types of things happened in the Bible when people ignored God and refused to learn His ways. Romans 6:23 says, "For the wages which sin pays is death."

If we look back at Jeremiah 4:20, we discover that "the whole land is laid waste; suddenly are my tents spoiled and destroyed..." Homes are broken up—mothers and fathers are divorcing, fathers are turning against sons, daughters are turning against mothers. This verse continues by saying, "Suddenly are my tents spoiled and destroyed, and my [tent] curtains ruined in a moment."

When you walk in rebellion, everything can be going great, and you can have it all together. But I am a witness of the fact that it can be brought down in a second.

> [O Lord] how long must I see the flag [marking the route for flight] and hear the sound of the trumpet [urging the people to flee for refuge]? [Their chastisement will continue until it has accomplished its purpose] for My people are stupid, says the Lord [replying to Jeremiah]; they do not know and understand Me. They are thickheaded children, and they have no understanding. They are wise to do evil, but to do good they have no knowledge [and know not how].
> —JEREMIAH 4:21–22

We have knowledge about doing good, but we do not know how to do it. The know-how to "do good" requires a combination of a new heart and a transformed mind. The heart understands, and the mind knows. When both are in operation, the good in the heart flows to the mind and trains it with "know-how" to live according to God's Word. This renewed mind passes on the manifestation to the physical body.

The Lord is saying from Jeremiah 5:22–23:

> Do you not fear and reverence Me? says the Lord. Do you not tremble before Me? I placed the sand for the boundary of the sea, a perpetual barrier beyond which it cannot pass and by an everlasting ordinance beyond which it cannot go? And though the waves of the sea toss and shake themselves, yet they cannot prevail [against the feeble grains of sand which God has ordained, by nature to be sufficient for His purpose]; though [the billows] roar, yet they cannot pass over that [barrier]. [Is not such a God to be reverently feared and worshiped?] But these people have hearts that draw back from God and wills that rebel against Him; they have revolted and quit His service and have gone away [into idolatry].

According to His sovereign will, God has ordained that small things can overcome the mighty—because everything is in His hand. However, as we learned in chapter one, the problem is that our priorities are out of order. Many of us still have an old heart, so we cannot love God or fear Him unto obedience.

Divine Warnings

> Say to them, Thus says the Lord, the God of Israel: Cursed is the man who does not heed the words of this covenant or solemn pledge which I commanded your fathers at the time that I brought them out of the land of Egypt, from the iron furnace, saying, Listen to My voice and do according to all that I command you. So will you be My people, and I will be your God, that I may perform the oath which I swore to your fathers, to give them a land flowing with milk and honey.
>
> —JEREMIAH 11:3–5

God does not want us to be destroyed. He does not desire for us to be tormented by the ways of this world. Instead, He gives His people divine warnings to get their attention and to compel them to change their ways. Jeremiah records His warning to the people in verses 5–7:

> Then I answered, Amen (so be it), O Lord. And the Lord said to me, Proclaim all these words in the cities of Judah and in the streets of Jerusalem: Hear the words of this covenant or solemn pledge and do them. For I earnestly protested and warned your fathers at the time that I brought them up *out of the land of Egypt...*
>
> —EMPHASIS ADDED

Do you see this? God never releases judgment without first sending a warning. This is why He is warning us, right now. He is telling us, "It is time to receive a new heart."

> ...even to this day, protesting to and warning them persistently, saying, Obey My voice. Yet they did not obey or incline their ear [to Me], but everyone walked in the stubbornness of his own evil heart. Therefore I brought upon them all [the calamities threatened in] the words of this covenant or solemn pledge, which I had commanded, but they did not do.
>
> —JEREMIAH 11:7–8

When that time comes...when God sends a "miracle" from the spirit realm that allows us to escape the old heart and we disobey His voice, He has no alternative. If we rebel against Him, we will reap disaster, just as Jerusalem did. Verse 11 says:

> Therefore thus says the Lord: Behold, I am bringing evil and calamity upon them which they will not be able to escape.

God is saying, "I warned you when I sent you the Word of God and revealed to you how to get out of it, but you disobeyed Me."

Divine warnings are the advance symptoms of heart failure. Therefore, when you receive a divine warning, *you know* when it is time for a change of heart. You know when that old heart is starting to break down.

Did you know that in today's medical industry it is virtually impossible to receive a new heart unless the old heart fails you? You cannot get a new heart until the old one breaks down—until it is starting to destroy your life. Then, and only then, will doctors recommend you for a heart transplant. Even in the natural realm, new hearts are in short supply.

Examine your heart right now. Ask yourself, "Is my heart destroying my life?" If so, you are a *candidate* for a heart transplant…but it does not stop there. You have to get up and go to the doctor in order to receive treatment. The doctor does not have a way of knowing that you need a heart transplant. You have to initiate the treatment, or the doctor cannot help you.

God is saying, "I warned you when I sent you the Word of God and revealed to you how to get out of it, but you disobeyed Me."

When I arrived at the emergency room, I had to go through Admitting before they could treat me. I had to go through the process—sign the papers, tell them my name, address and what my problem was. I had to "confess" these things before the doctor could help me. Are you seeing the revelation?

Lamentations 1:20 says:

> Behold, O Lord, how distressed I am! My vital parts (emotions) are in tumult and are deeply disturbed; my heart cannot rest and is violently agitated within me, for I have grievously rebelled. Outside the house the sword bereaves, at home there is [famine, pestilence] death!

In other words, when I go out or when I am at home, I am being attacked. There is no relief.

> [My foes] have heard that I [Jerusalem] sigh
> and groan, that I have no comforter [in You].
> All my enemies have heard of my trouble; they
> are glad [O Lord] that You have done it. You will
> bring the day [of Judah's punishment] that you
> have foretold and proclaimed; [it involves also
> my foes' punishment] and they will become like
> me. Let all their wickedness come before You;
> and deal with them as You have dealt with me
> because of all of my transgressions; for my sighs
> and groans are many and my heart is faint.
>
> —LAMENTATIONS 1:21–22

The most powerful sign of your need for a new
heart is these four golden words: *"My heart is faint."*
God's vital signs of breakdown will bring you to this
place. *This is God's heart*—that you would understand and know that you need a new heart. He is
waiting for you to say, "I cannot survive with this old
heart. It has destroyed everything around me. It is
destroying everything within me, and the number
one thing that I cannot bear is the fact that I find no
comfort in You, God. You are not my Comforter, so
how can I survive without You?"

When that is the cry of your heart, God is telling
you that you need a new heart.

Chapter 6

A Scientific
Point of View

Have you ever used something for a long time before you read the directions? Then when you read them, you discovered how it should *really work* and how much more that thing was capable of (than what you knew). After using it according to the directions, you became amazed at what you had been doing right all the time, and also at what you had missed that kept you from using it to its fullest potential.

When I started studying about the heart and brain, I was literally amazed—at times shocked into silence. More than this, I stood in awe of God, realizing how incredibly He has built us. As we move forward in this chapter you are going to see the Word of God being confirmed over and over again in brand-new ways.

Like me, I pray that you will give God the glory and honor that He deserves. I pray that by learning these incredible truths, your love for Him will grow deeper. We are truly "fearfully and wonderfully made" (Ps. 139:14, KJV). David also said in this verse,

"Marvellous are thy works; and that my soul knoweth right well." Understanding God's works changed his soul! It can change yours.

I pray that, like me, you will read on and say to God, "I lay my life—*everything that I am*—down at Your feet." I pray that you will ask Him for a new heart.

The new heart transformation is very scriptural, as you have been able to see as you read the previous chapters. Everything that God does (in the spirit realm) has an explanation, symbol or example in the natural realm.

> But it is not the spiritual life which came first, but the physical and then the spiritual. The first man [was] from out of earth, made of dust (earthly-minded); the second Man [is] the Lord from out of heaven. Now those who are made of the dust are like him who was first made of the dust (earthly-minded); and as is [the Man] from heaven, so also [are those] who are of heaven (heavenly-minded). And just as we have borne the image [of the man] of dust, so shall we and so let us also bear the image [of the Man] of heaven.
>
> —1 CORINTHIANS 15:46–49

When you look at what scientists have discovered about the heart, you will be amazed at how far behind the eight ball believers *really are*. The secular world has gained a thorough understanding of the heart's anatomy and functions, explaining it to the point that believers can look at the information from scientists and know that it had to be revealed to *them* by God.

God is so determined for us to get this message that when He could not find anybody in the Christian world to seek Him long enough—to get in His presence to receive the revelation—He revealed it to scientists so that we (His children) could understand what He is trying to tell us about this new heart.

The Natural Heart

Allow me to start by giving you a few "heart facts." The heart generally functions for seventy to eighty years without maintenance or replacement. During this time, it beats around one hundred thousand times a day, roughly forty million times a year—almost three billion beats in a lifetime. The heart pumps two gallons of blood per minute, adding up to more than one hundred gallons per hour, through a vascular system that is long enough to wrap around the earth two times—over sixty thousand miles. That powerful organ sits inside of each person.[1]

The heart is like a nuclear power plant. It generates five thousand times more energy than the brain. This is one of the main reasons why the heart has been called the "center" of our being. Even more amazing, it has its own nervous system that is called the "brain of the heart." This "heart brain" has more than forty thousand nerve cells, the same number of cells contained in many of the brain's subcortical centers. Research has proven that the heart brain can and does act independently of the brain in your head![2]

The heart can even beat without being connected to the brain. For example, when someone has a heart transplant, the surgeons have to sever the nerves that run from the brain to the heart. When they put the heart into the new body, they do not yet know how to reconnect the nerves. So the surgeons restore the heartbeat, and it keeps beating—even though there is no "nerve" connection to the brain.[3]

When heart rhythms are in balance, like a mighty waterfall, it releases a balanced flow that resonates throughout our being.

The natural heart is also able to feel, sense, learn and remember. From this, scientists have also observed that the heart sends emotional and intuitive signals to the brain and body that help to govern our lives.

The heart produces a strong substance called "atrial natriuretic factor" (ANF) or atrial peptide, nicknamed "the balance hormone," that "regulates" many of our brain's functions—as well as our organs.[4] Scientists are now finding that the balance hormone also motivates our behavior.[5] The heart's power center directs and aligns many of our bodies' systems and helps them to function in harmony. When heart rhythms are in balance, like a mighty waterfall, it releases a balanced flow that resonates throughout our being.

Heart Vision

~∿∾~

The light of the body is the eye: if therefore
thine eye be single, thy whole body shall be full
of light.

—MATTHEW 6:22, KJV

The word *eye* means "vision."[6] The word *single*
means "folded together...to twine or braid."[7] How can
we achieve this balanced, complete vision? How can
we see from a heavenly perspective, according to the
Word of God? We must be born again and receive a
new heart, which causes heavenly vision to flow from
the center of our being to our brains and throughout
the rest of our bodies.

The heart is the center of our understanding—
where concepts and balanced intelligence are intro-
duced to every part of us. It can send waves of rational,
considerate instruction to the brain. If the busy brain
receives this instruction, it brings a balanced perspective, which can strengthen our conscience. However,
the old heart does not have the spiritual power to override the brain's constant activity. This is why even our
human conscience can be deceived.

For example, let us look at John 8 where the
scribes and Pharisees brought a woman to Jesus who
had been caught in the act of adultery. The religious
leaders reminded Him of the Law—she should be
put to death (vv. 3–5). After listening to their argu-
ment, finally Jesus stood up (from where He had
been writing in the dirt) and said to them, "He that
is without sin among you, let him first cast a stone at
her" (v. 7, KJV).

Suddenly their consciences kicked in: "And they which heard it, being convicted by their own conscience, went out one by one, beginning at the eldest, even unto the last: and Jesus was left alone, and the woman standing in the midst" (v. 9, KJV). The Word from Jesus' mouth penetrated their "old hearts" and revealed their hypocrisy—so they left with their old hearts intact. How do I know this?

Their old hearts could understand their own guilt, but they did not have the power to convert and save their souls! They had enough "conscience" to convict someone else of sin, but they still did not have the ability to repent and ask Jesus to give them a new heart. Why? Titus 1:15–16 says:

> To the pure [in heart and conscience] all things are pure, but to the defiled and corrupt and unbelieving nothing is pure; their very minds and consciences are defiled and polluted. They profess to know God [to recognize, perceive, and be acquainted with Him], but deny and disown and renounce Him by what they do; they are detestable and loathsome, unbelieving and disobedient and disloyal and rebellious, and [they are] unfit and worthless for good work (deed or enterprise) of any kind.

The scribes and Pharisees had a "form" of godliness, but they denied His power. They were in the full swing of deception. They had become people pleasers—comparing themselves *by* themselves. They had forgotten that they were God's children and should *serve* others, not *crucify* them. As a result the Israelites could not look at their leaders and see their Savior—because these leaders had not pursued the new heart. Therefore, no matter what they did, these leaders could not please God.

It takes a pure, new heart to create a pure, undefiled conscience. The revelation does not stop there. Jesus turned to the woman in John 8 and gave her the solution: "'I am the light of the world: he that followeth me shall not walk in darkness, but shall have the light of life" (v. 12, KJV). In other words, He was saying, "The men who accused you were walking in the deception of their own, darkened, earthly consciences. But I am able to give you a new heart that will fill your mind, and every part of you, with light—a balanced, complete, heavenly vision and understanding." That is powerful!

The heart understands, and the mind knows. This is why the Book of Proverbs, the book of wisdom, opens with these words:

> The Proverbs (truths obscurely expressed, maxims, and parables) of Solomon son of David, king of Israel: that people may know skillful and godly Wisdom and instruction, discern and comprehend the words of understanding and insight, receive instruction in wise dealing and the discipline of wise thoughtfulness, righteousness, justice, and integrity, that prudence may be given to the simple, and knowledge, discretion, and discernment to the youth.
>
> —PROVERBS 1:1–4

Throughout the Bible, the line of distinction is drawn between "knowing" and "understanding" because there is a distinct difference.

The Natural Mind

~~∽~~

The brain begins to develop after the heart is formed. It grows from the bottom up—the brain stem (medulla oblongata), emotional center (amygdala) and then the logic centers (cerebral cortex and frontal lobes).

The medulla contains the nerve systems that regulate our heart rate, breathing and other body functions. This means that the first part of the brain is created to link it with the heart and to direct or adjust how fast it beats. It monitors and facilitates communication to the heart, lungs, nervous system and parts of the body.

The amygdala develops next. It stores emotional memories and compares these experiences with new information. It determines what is relevant to each individual and forms the brain's basis for our perceptions. As the brain develops, it grows out of this emotional center to develop our logical capabilities. This is why what we perceive and what is *real* can be two different things. It is also why our imagination, strategies and decisions are colored by our emotions. When emotions are balanced, they give life and meaning to facts, objectives and logic. When unbalanced, they distort the truth.

The third section of the brain, the cerebral cortex, develops next. It reasons and reflects, evaluates and considers, strategizes, plans and imagines. It takes the relevant information passed on from the amygdala and makes sense out of it. It can also make nonsense out of it if the imagination goes wild. Whether balanced or unbalanced, this information gets passed on to the next brain center.

The frontal lobes are the fourth, and final, section of the brain. This is where our decision making is done. The lobes also determine which emotional response is appropriate for each situation. It feeds from the emotions and sends the updated instructions back to the emotions.[8]

God created the heart to govern the brain. The heart is outside of the brain and, technically, is not subject to brain processes. However, when we choose to ignore our heart's direction, the brain assumes control. It takes over, operating from a linear and logical perspective, always ready to defend its own interests. The brain has no understanding, so it is territorial—nothing foreign (spiritual) can enter without a fight.

The brain is always active, even while you are sleeping, trying to get your attention through dreams. It stays in a position of alertness to defend or attack when it, or your body, senses a threat—real or perceived—to its existence and development.

The brain tries to pass on information to the heart, but the heart does not have to accept it. And this is where we encounter the mystery of the new heart. Logically, our old heart (by virtue of how God created it) should be able to override the brain. However, Adam and Eve perverted this ability when they followed their brains instead of their hearts (the enemy's great deception) in the Garden of Eden (Gen. 3). Now, in order to balance and control the mind, we must receive the new heart.

As our brains form perceptions and react to the

outside world, neural messages travel down through the medulla that can affect the rhythms of our hearts. The heart, however, has been designed to send messages back to the brain. (Scientists have already observed that the brain both identifies and obeys these messages!) The new heart can filter life-giving information to the brain that not only alters our consciousness, but also our actions.

It has also been medically proven that when we focus on our hearts, the balance of the functions between the heart and brain increases.[9] When this synchronization takes place, every other bodily function operates to its fullest capacity. When we focus attention on our brains, however, our whole body comes under stress and falls out of balance. Maybe that is why stress has been called "the silent killer." It is a matter of the heart—the choice is yours.

Jesus said that unless we become simple, like a child, we cannot enter His kingdom (Mark 10:15). We have to reject our logic and emotions, and with wide-open eyes, turn around and embrace the spiritual truth that flows from our new hearts.

> The law of the Lord is perfect, restoring the [whole] person; the testimony of the Lord is sure, making wise the simple. The precepts of the Lord are right, rejoicing the heart; the commandment of the Lord is pure and bright, enlightening the eyes. The [reverent] fear of the Lord is clean, enduring forever; the ordinances of the Lord are true and righteous altogether.
>
> More to be desired are they than gold, even than much fine gold; they are sweeter also than honey and drippings from the honeycomb. Moreover, by them is Your servant warned

(reminded, illuminated, and instructed); and in keeping them there is great reward. Who can discern his lapses and errors? Clear me from hidden [and unconscious] faults. Keep back Your servant also from presumptuous sins; let them not have dominion over me! Then shall I be blameless, and I shall be innocent and clear of great transgression. Let the words of my mouth and the meditation of my heart be acceptable in Your sight, O Lord, my [firm, impenetrable] Rock and my Redeemer.

—PSALM 19:7–14

Formation of the Heart and Mind

Let us go back to the genesis of the heart and mind in a human fetus. When a child is conceived in the mother's womb, the first thing that develops is a heartbeat. After determining that a woman is pregnant, the heartbeat is the first thing the doctor goes after. He does not examine the mother, first looking for the eyes, nose, brain and nervous system. He listens for a heartbeat, and if there is a heartbeat, the child is alive.

People who live from old heart reasoning—including pro-choice advocates—believe that life does not begin until the brain is functioning. But people who listen to and obey their new heart understand that the heart is where life begins. In fact, the heart begins to store its memory code from being connected to the mother's umbilical cord.

Expectant mothers are told to talk gently and lovingly to their unborn child and to gently stroke the outside of their womb. These words and actions are recorded into that child's memory code before it is ever born. When the child is birthed out into the world, he or she already has a record of everything that it has experienced since its first heartbeat.

As that baby begins to grow, by the time that child is six months old, the record of its experiences has escalated at an unbelievable rate. This is where the problem begins—the heart inside a six-month-old baby has already had six months' accumulation of memories in the world. That baby's brain, with its four different sections, is constantly being fed instant information from society. Already, more information is coming into the brain than the immature heart can handle. Because the brain is receiving more information than the heart can process, the brain "perceives" that it should govern that heart and body.

Remember that our hearts also have a "brain," which integrates and processes intuitive information and signals from the brain and body. However, it is young and already out-of-balance because of the sin nature it inherited from Adam and Eve's fall. Coupled with this, the body and the brain are exposed the most to society. When the brain sends constant information to that young heart, the heart tries to process it (in order to regulate the response), but the brain keeps bombarding it with more and more information—which leaves the young heart miles behind.

This sets the pattern that runs throughout our lifetimes unless we receive the new heart. By the time our hearts can process new information, the brain has already sent messages to the body, and both body and brain have responded to *knowledge*—the way that the world handles things—and not to heart understanding. This puts the old heart in constant jeopardy of spiritual heart failure.

The next stage of a Christian's development is the formative years. Psychologists have proven that, without fail, by the time a child reaches five years of age, his or her heart and mind patterns are basically set for life. This same stage applies to our spiritual lives. It is imperative—especially during the first five years of your walk with God—that you spend time in the Word, worship and prayer in order to transform your mind.

> # The heart must be converted before you can have a change of mind and a new perspective.

The converted heart longs to walk in the ways of God, which means that it "declares war" on the resident mind. Then the spiritual battle begins:

> Do not be conformed to this world (this age), [fashioned after and adapted to its external, superficial customs], but be transformed (changed) by the [entire] renewal of your mind [by its new ideals and its new attitude], so that you may prove [for yourselves] what is the good and acceptable and perfect will of God, even the thing which is good and acceptable and perfect [in His sight for you].
>
> —ROMANS 12:2

When you are more mature, have learned your heart's rhythm and experienced what happens when you react to information that has been "spit out" by the brain—real or perceived—the results you have suffered teach you not to do that again. However, young Christian hearts have the greatest battle. They are birthed into the church and know the Lord, but the information from the brain still over-flows their hearts. (This also happens to saints who refuse to be weaned from the "milk" of the Word. They cannot grow up to eat the "bread," and then the "meat," of the Word.)

With heart and brain unified (aligned), you will experience a natural flow, rhythm and peace within—no matter what is going on in the natural world.

You do not have to wonder anymore why we are so tuned into our thought patterns and why we let our minds govern our lives. As I said before, we are living in a brain world. The information our brains receive tells us that we can change our heart and change our lives if we change our mind. This is not what God intended. The mind does not *change*. It jealously fights to keep everything "the way it has always been." The heart must be converted before you can have a change of mind and a new perspective.

The mind needs to be retrained with the

understanding that is built into the new heart—
which is the heart of God. The mind must be
retrained through the Word of God. Then the emotional and rational memory banks will be refilled
with godly information from the Bible.

Synergy of Heart and Mind

The new heart and the renewed mind are a powerful
combination. When understanding flows from the
heart to the renewed mind, it identifies with what is
already there and causes the body to receive the
blessing. The mind is first "emotional," so the Word
of God must enter the amygdala on a constant basis
and create an emotional connection to the heart of
God within you. Then, and only then, will your decisions be balanced by God's Word. Light and harmony will flood your entire being. With heart and
brain unified (aligned), you will experience a natural
flow, rhythm and peace within—no matter what is
going on in the natural world.

Jesus exemplified this uncommon existence. The
apostle Paul describes this existence and instructs
us to seek the same for ourselves:

> Let this same attitude and purpose and [hum-
> ble] mind be in you which was in Christ Jesus:
> [Let Him be your example in humility:] Who,
> although being essentially one with God and in
> the form of God [possessing the fullness of the
> attributes which make God God], did not think
> this equality with God was a thing to be eagerly
> grasped or retained, but stripped Himself [of all
> privileges and rightful dignity], so as to assume

the guise of a servant (slave), in that He became like men and was born a human being.

And after He had appeared in human form, He abased and humbled Himself [still further] and carried His obedience to the extreme of death, even the death of the cross! Therefore [because He stooped so low] God has highly exalted Him and has freely bestowed on Him the name that is above every name. That in (at) the name of Jesus every knee should (must) bow, in heaven and on earth and under the earth, and every tongue [frankly and openly] confess and acknowledge that Jesus Christ is Lord, to the glory of God the Father.

—PHILIPPIANS 2:5–11

This "Christ-life" existence takes us back to giving up our right to "be right," because this is what Jesus did. When He humbled Himself in obedience to God, His name became something that Satan recognized as power.

We cannot let the mind control us. We must ask for a new heart and then begin to obey the divine messages that God sends from within us. When we do, we will walk in divine authority because we will be in sync with the way God intended us to be. And when we are in sync with what God intended, the devil has to flee from us when we resist him (James 4:7).

When you have been born again, you may constantly look for and seek God in prayer for anointing and authority over the enemy because you do not understand that you already have the power to defeat him within you. The only thing that gives you control over the enemy is the synergy of the new heart and a renewed mind that is fully submitted to God and His will.

When your mind is submitted to the will of God, which flows from your new heart, then this heart begins to rule and dominate your flesh and influence your surroundings. Since God resides in your new heart, and the character of God is already in it, you are automatically placed in a seat above Satan! You do not have to pray to get there. Your new heart transforms you to your rightful place. As you surrender your mind on a daily basis, it keeps you there.

The only thing that gives you control over the enemy is the synergy of the new heart and a renewed mind that is fully submitted to God and His will.

Jesus came to the earth with the heart of God inside of Him. He still, however, could have aborted His assignment if He made the wrong choices. He could have walked around, allowing His mind to dictate what He did or did not do and what He had the right to be. Since He was the Son of God, He could have demanded to be given a mansion, servants, wealth and everything else—and it all would have happened—but He didn't. He chose, instead, to obey His Father's heart.

Jesus came into the earth with a dying heart. His goal was to die—to fulfill an eternal assignment. His converted heart was built with an assignment already in it. He submitted to His heart and obeyed the will of the Father, which already resided there.

When we are born again and receive the new heart, it comes with an assignment already in it. We need to do what Jesus did instead of letting our minds and bodies dictate what we have "the right" to do and be. We can let *go* and *let God*.

Our heavenly Father is saying, "I want you to submit to obedience, because when you give up your right to 'be right' in the natural realm, your new heart will govern what you do from the spirit realm, and that is when you will have victory. That is when you will receive power to do what Jesus did."

God is telling us like never before—*we need a new heart.*

Chapter 7

Results of a **Heart Transplant**

We have learned how the old heart is conceived and developed, and that it forms the basis of who we are. Now we will take a look at it from another angle. We all have a natural heart, but not many have new hearts that they have received from God. In the natural realm, when a surgeon says that a heart transplant is necessary, it is a matter of life and death.

> ## The new heart brings new warfare because the enemy wants to keep you bound and ineffective.

This is the same in the spiritual realm. God has already said that the heart "is exceedingly perverse and corrupt and severely, mortally sick! Who can know it [perceive, understand, be acquainted with his own heart and mind]?" (Jer. 17:9). We desperately need a spiritual heart transplant!

God has already provided a Donor for all who desire to undergo this vital procedure. The heart that rested inside of Jesus is available for transplant into your life. It is a heart of power. Jesus' heart came with an eternal assignment—and when we receive His heart, we receive our part of that mission. But just as the person who receives a transplanted natural heart must engage in a fight to keep his or her body from rejecting that transplanted heart, so too the enemy fights us tooth-and-nail to try to make us reject our new heart. He knows that the only way he can delay or cause us to abort our divine assignment is to cause us to reject our new heart. The new heart brings new warfare because the enemy wants to keep you bound and ineffective.

The new heart sets us free, dresses us for battle and puts us right back into active duty.

Whether you have realized it or not, there has always been a battle for your soul. Sadly, many of us have functioned like prisoners of war. Stripped of our weapons and uniforms, the enemy has chained us and thrown us into a pit of bondage. There is little to no food (Word) there, and there is definitely no rest. The enemy's cruel forced labor drains every ounce of your strength. The new heart sets us free, dresses us for battle and puts us right back into active duty.

Some spiritual POWs never overcome the trauma of war. Even after they have been rescued and brought back home, their minds torment them with reruns of what used to be. Though they have been set free, they are spiritually paralyzed. Through torment and deception, the enemy has disabled them. They do not even try to walk in their newfound freedom. They need a new heart—just like the generation of Israelites who died in the wilderness because they were afraid to obey God's voice (Num. 32:13).

A Divine Charge

When you receive a new heart, you can expect a battle. Your flesh, and the outside world, will not give up control without a fight. When God spoke to the Israelites, who because of the continual disobedience flowing out of their old hearts and unrenewed minds had been taken captive and scattered out of the Promised Land, He gave them a divine charge:

> Therefore say, Thus says the Lord God: I will gather you from the peoples and assemble you out of the countries where you have been scattered, and I will give back to you the land of Israel. And when they return there, they shall take away from it all traces of its detestable things and all its abominations (sex impurities and heathen religious practices). And I will give them one heart [a new heart] and I will put a new spirit within them; and I will take the stony [unnaturally hardened] heart out of their flesh, and will give them a heart of flesh [sensitive and responsive to the touch of their God].
>
> —EZEKIEL 11:17–19

God promised to gather His people and to give them back their land. But it wouldn't be without a fight! Along with their new heart would come the courage to take possession of their land and clean out all the impurities.

When Jesus talked with His own followers about living the "Christ life" with their new hearts, He said:

> If the world hates you, know that it hated Me before it hated you. If you belonged to the world, the world would treat you with affection and would love you as its own. But because you are not of the world [no longer one with it], but I have chosen (selected) you out of the world, the world hates (detests) you. Remember that I told you, A servant is not greater than his master [is not superior to him].
>
> —JOHN 15:18–20

The good news is that Jesus overcame the world (John 16:33). He died to give us a healthy, new heart, and when that heart is transplanted inside of us, we have part of Jesus—the One who died and rose again—in our innermost being!

Every memory Jesus has of the Father, from before the foundation of the world, is inside of you. His experiences of walking with power and authority on earth and casting Satan down are stored in your new heart. Memories of when He rose from the dead and then ascended to sit on the right hand of the Father flow through your veins. Everything that God is—*since the dawn of eternity*—lives inside of you. If you have a new heart, you have supernatural power! The question is, *If we have truly received this new heart, how can we fail?*

If we trust and obey our new heart, Jesus will help us to get rid of all the "detestable things" and "abominations." Philippians 1:6 says:

> And I am convinced and sure of this very thing, that He Who began a good work in you will continue until the day of Jesus Christ [right up to the time of His return], developing [that good work] and perfecting and bringing it to full completion in you.

In other words, Jesus will work inside of you until you do consistently what is pleasing to God (Phil. 2:13). If you obey the Lord, your new heart will lead you through this life and into eternity. It is actually your *deposit* of eternity, because Christ has already passed through death and ascended to heaven.

> He has made everything beautiful in its time. He also has planted eternity in men's hearts and minds [a divinely implanted sense of a purpose working through the ages which nothing under the sun but God alone can satisfy], yet so that men cannot find out what God has done from the beginning to the end.
>
> —ECCLESIASTES 3:11

God has an *appointed time* and a *purpose* for you on the earth. The only way you will fulfill that purpose and assignment is to trust and obey Him.

> Therefore also now, says the Lord, turn and keep on coming to Me with all your heart, with fasting, with weeping, and with mourning [until every hindrance is removed and the broken fellowship is restored]. Rend your hearts and not your garments and return to the Lord, your

God, for He is gracious and merciful, slow to
anger, and abounding in loving-kindness; and
He revokes His sentence of evil [when His con-
ditions are met].

—JOEL 2:12–13

A Divine Transition

~◠~

If you set six different pendulum clocks close together
and start them swaying at different times, ultimately
they all come into alignment—swaying in the same
direction and on the same beat. Scientists call this
process entrainment.

> ## The question is, *If we have truly received this new heart, how can we fail?*

In your physical body, your most powerful organ
will pull the others into its force of energy. It is the
same in the spirit realm. Your new heart, being the
heart of God, has infinitely more power than anything else does. Change will come if you allow it. Are
you ready to change?

Though powerful, the old heart has been over-
programmed (by the brain) from birth. Its natural
rhythm has been distorted, so it pulls everything
into an out-of-sync pattern. It does not maintain a
healthy balance. Organs are in place but not functioning the way they should. That is why we need

a new heart. We need the Lord to help us put everything into balance.

> Diverse and deceitful weights are shamefully vile and abhorrent to the Lord, and false scales are not good.
>
> —PROVERBS 20:23

Your new heart has been designed to clear out everything that is unbalanced and deceitful. This transplant moves you from *one place* to *another place*. It changes you, step by step, from one stage into another. God is moving you toward your new assignment. Things may feel strange at first, but if you will submit to God, He will do His "perfect work" in you (2 Tim. 3:16–17; James 1:4).

Since your new heart is no longer connected to your brain, it lives totally from the power of God! It receives its "messages" from the "information" that has been stored deep in His heart. Whatever is programmed in your new heart when God sets it into your chest cavity is the assignment that you will begin to carry out.

"Natural" Heart Transitions

I recently read a story about a girl who received the heart of another young girl who had been murdered. The murder case could not be solved, so the police had closed the case. Months later the little girl began to have dreams and visions about the incident— down to the smallest detail. When she told her mother, they filed a report with the police, describing the man who killed her donor—down to where he lived. She even told them what the little girl had said to her killer. The murderer was arrested.[1] It is amazing, but true. The donor's heart held that vital information and passed it on to its new mind and body.

I heard another story from a syndicated radio program where they were interviewing a doctor who specializes in heart transplant case studies. He shared that he had talked with a man who started having a recurring dream after his heart transplant. Over and over again he saw a young woman who had fallen to her death down a flight of stairs. Troubled, he came to the doctor, and they started tracing the origins of his new heart. They discovered that the donor's daughter had fallen down a flight of stairs and died from a broken neck.[2]

There are many other stories of strange things happening when people received new hearts, including changes in appetite and relationship changes. The important thing to remember is that your new heart will create change that your mind cannot control.

The new heart stops taking the "information overload" from your old brain because it does not need it. It functions from the miracle power of God. He will begin to purge those things from within you that do not line up with His Word.

> Consider it wholly joyful, my brethren, whenever you are enveloped in or encounter trials of any sort or fall into various temptations. Be assured and understand that the trial and proving of your faith bring out endurance and steadfastness and patience. But let endurance and steadfastness and patience have full play and do a thorough work, so that you may be [people]

perfectly and fully developed [with no defects], lacking in nothing.

—JAMES 1:2–4

The Mind Declares War

~⌒~

The new heart has come to assume its rightful place of authority, and the brain is painfully aware of this. Scientists have said that the brain *fears* the heart, and I believe this is especially so once it is severed from its nerve connection.[3] The old mind knows that Someone else is in control. The new assignment in that heart is going to be fulfilled—with or without the brain's help.

When we are no longer obeying the old mind, it is being put to death. A paradigm shift is occurring. While the old mind is being put to death (as the result of reading and obeying God's Word), the new heart is replacing the old actions and patterns in the brain. As you sow to the Spirit, it is taking back the ground that Satan once occupied.

The mind perceives this as a threat to its existence, so it declares war on the new heart...and the battles continue. The apostle Paul said:

> So I find it to be a law (rule of action of my being) that when I want to do what is right and good, evil is ever present with me and I am subject to its insistent demands. For I endorse and delight in the Law of God in my inmost self [with my new nature]. But I discern in my bodily members [in the sensitive appetites and wills of the flesh] a different law (rule of action) at war against the law of my mind (my reason) and

making me a prisoner to the law of sin that
dwells in my bodily organs [in the sensitive
appetites and wills of the flesh].

—ROMANS 7:21–23

The mind is used to speeding, racing and responding to the worldly way of doing things. In other
words, if you walk up to me and slap me, then my
brain says, "I have been trained by society to slap
you back."

But the new heart says, "Turn the other cheek." It
tells you, "If a person wants your coat, give him your
cloak also." The new heart tells us to walk a mile for
peace (Matt. 5:39–41).

When an enemy comes against you and wounds
you, the old mind says, "I do not want to have anything to do with you."

But the Word that flows from the new heart says,
"Love your enemies, bless them that curse you, do
good to them that hate you, and pray for them which
despitefully use you" (Matt. 5:44, KJV). So you enter
into immediate warfare, because the Word of God is
piercing that old mind and literally "canceling out"
worldly thought patterns.

A Two-Pronged Counterattack

When you obey the new heart's rulership, the Word
actually begins to renew the mind from without and
from within. The brain is sandwiched. You have the
Word *inside* of you and are putting the Word *into*
you (from outside) by reading the Bible—which
travels through your eyes and goes directly to the

brain! So the old heart pattern is literally being squeezed out. That is why the battle rages and you feel the conflict inside of you. Your thought patterns have been "dug in" for years and years.

It is important to understand the process of receiving the new heart. It begins one day as you sit in a church service. Someone asks you if you want to be saved, and you go to the altar and receive the new heart. At that moment, everything changes, sending signals to the brain that it is going to die. The first explosion goes off in the mind, which hates being out of control. It loathes being disconnected.

That is why the battle rages and you feel the conflict inside of you. Your thought patterns have been "dug in" for years and years.

Even as you kneel at the altar deciding to follow Christ, thoughts begin to dart through your mind: *I cannot give this up. I am not ready to do this. I am afraid that So-and-so will not understand.* This is your first battle in the war of your new heart. Your mind continues to perceive and conceive evil, but it does not have an old heart into which to plant the evil anymore. The new heart does not need the brain's input. It will not receive that earthly garbage. It is connected to eternity.

So the mind keeps throwing out its "alarm signals" to the flesh, for the body to obey its instructions and carry out the ungodly actions. The new heart responds by sending a wave of conviction, and the battle goes on. Soon the flesh determines that it no longer enjoys the assignment it has received from the mind because the new heart is convicting it.

Do Not Quench the Spirit

In 1970, Doctors John and Beatrice Lacey observed the following phenomenon. They were able to document that when the brain sent alarm signals to the body, the heart did not automatically obey (as did the other organs). While the other organs began to function in an alarm state, the heart would continue to beat slowly. Not only this, but they also observed that the heart appeared to be sending messages back to the brain, which the brain not only understood, but also obeyed. They even documented that it appeared that these heart messages could influence a person's "motivated behavior."[4]

> Your new heart will bring you to a *valley of decision* as you go through the process of purification.

Your new heart is a powerful, yet gentle ruler. If you submit to its promptings in spite of your brain's resistance, the heart will send a message back to the brain that says, "I am not going to do it that way. I am not going to answer that way." As you submit to God, these messages will become so powerful that the body will divorce the brainwaves and begin to line up with your new heart. This is not just a spiritual truth; it is a physical fact.

If the heart sends a clear, intuitive signal with a feeling that says, "Don't do this," the head may vigorously resist, demanding to know "Why? How? When?" so persistently that the heart's signal is cut off.[5] In Christendom, we call this "quenching the Spirit." This can also explain why it can be so difficult at times to pray or enter into true, heartfelt worship. First Thessalonians 5:19 says, "Do not quench (suppress or subdue) the [Holy] Spirit."

God continues to purge the "detestable things" in our flesh as we read and obey His Word. Everything "hidden" begins to be exposed and discarded as the Word digs up each impure thought and motive. Your battle will be to submit to the Spirit's direction, and this can be an awesome fight. If you do not submit to your new heart, ultimately you will be stripped by the enemy and thrown into a cold, dark place. Your new heart will bring you to a *valley of decision* as you go through the process of purification.

For example, if you read the scripture (outside information coming into your mind) that says, "Love thy neighbor as thyself," and your new heart (information from the heart of Christ) is already programmed to love your neighbor, when the evil thought arises to say, "Hate your neighbor," it will be ineffective. The message *coming in* that says, "Love thy neighbor," combines with the new heart desire to love *already inside of you* and attacks that evil thought from both sides, squeezing it out. When you disobey, the opposite happens. Your heart becomes "faint" because you are rejecting it. (See Lamentations 1:20–22.)

God's Measuring Line

It is God who determines how well we are progressing on our transformation into the Christ-life after we receive our new hearts. When He brought His people out of captivity and returned them to the land of promise, He told them He was going to measure the progress they made on rebuilding His temple.

> Therefore say to them [the Jews of this day], Thus says the Lord of hosts: Return to Me, says the Lord of hosts, and I will return to you; it is the utterance of the Lord of hosts...So the angel who talked with me said to me, Cry out, Thus says the Lord of hosts: I am jealous for Jerusalem and for Zion with a great jealousy. And I am very angry with the nations that are at ease; for while I was but a little displeased, they helped forward the affliction and disaster. Therefore thus says the Lord: I have returned to Jerusalem with compassion (loving-kindness and mercy). My house shall be built in it, says the Lord of hosts, and a measuring line shall be stretched out over Jerusalem [with a view to rebuilding its walls].
>
> —ZECHARIAH 1:3, 14–16

When God begins to restore and construct the real temple within us, it will be done according to His measuring line, not our "false" weights and measures. This is why we desperately need the new heart. Verses 17–21 continue:

> Cry yet again, saying, Thus says the Lord of hosts: My cities shall yet again overflow with prosperity, and the Lord shall yet comfort Zion and shall yet choose Jerusalem. Then I lifted up my eyes and saw, and behold, four horns [symbols of strength]. And I said to the angel who talked with me, What are these? And he answered me, These are the horns or powers which have scattered Judah, Israel, and Jerusalem. Then the Lord showed me four smiths or workmen [one for each enemy horn, to beat it down]. Then said I, What are these [horns and smiths] coming to do? And He said, These are the horns or powers that scattered Judah so that no man lifted up his head. But these smiths or workmen have come to terrorize them and cause them to be panic-stricken, to cast out the horns or powers of the nations who lifted up their horn against the land of Judah to scatter it.

When we surrender our hearts to God and say, "No more!", He will do battle on our behalf. He has already prepared a host of angels to fight for us. He has also prepared the Holy Spirit to stretch out the "measuring rod," *so that this time* when we come to Him, we will be built properly. We will be constructed according to the right measurements and fulfill the purpose and assignment that He has already placed in our new heart.

> So shall My Word be that goes forth out of My
> mouth; it shall not return to Me void [without
> producing any effect, useless], but it shall
> accomplish that which I please and purpose, and
> it shall prosper in the thing for which I sent it.
>
> —ISAIAH 55:11

When God sends a Word from the abundance that
is in His heart, it always prospers. This is why we
must not reject the new heart. When "evil treasure"
is inside of you (in your old heart), you cannot
expect to *confess* good things and get what you
want! This is perversion, because you are doing
things exactly opposite of the way that God
intended. (See Jeremiah 17:9.)

> The upright (honorable, intrinsically good)
> man out of the good treasure [stored] in his
> heart produces what is upright (honorable and
> intrinsically good), and the evil man out of the
> evil storehouse brings forth that which is
> depraved (wicked and intrinsically evil); for out
> of the abundance (overflow) of the heart his
> mouth speaks.
>
> —LUKE 6:45

God searches our hearts. He knows when our
words come from the abundance of righteousness
that He has stored within us. And *these* words—not
the empty confessions from the brain—will yield
eternal results, and our Father will be pleased.

He is faithful to tell us when we are doing well, not
through somebody else's words and standards, but
by speaking directly to our new heart, saying, "Well
done, good and faithful servant" (Matt. 25:23, KJV).
God's voice is the only one that *really counts*.

We can compliment each other, compare our-selves against one another and say many things—but we must realize that many who encourage us are still "guppies" in the Spirit. They are not "big fish" to God. They just seem to be because they are stroking our flesh. According to God's measuring line, they are not where they need to be. The danger of comparison surfaces again! In the ocean, a guppy would be so tiny that it would say to a goldfish, "Oh, you are such a big, beautiful, bright fish!" A shark, on the other hand, would see it differently.

God's voice is the only one that *really counts*.

Let us not think of ourselves "more highly" than we ought to think (Rom. 12:3). We are utterly dependent upon God and the new heart that He puts within us. If we fail to trust and obey Him as He begins to purify our earthly temples, we can be taken prisoner again by the enemy. We can submit to God's rebuilding process, or we can go back to the pit. The choice is ours. We need to embrace the new heart.

Chapter 8

The New **Heart**

The new heart is an amazing mystery, and we must walk in the Spirit to understand its depths. We hold the feelings and purposes of God within us! That is awesome.

> For who has known or understood the mind (the counsels and purposes) of the Lord so as to guide and instruct Him and give Him knowledge? But we have the mind of Christ (the Messiah) and do hold the thoughts (feelings and purposes) of His heart.
>
> —1 CORINTHIANS 2:16

Even more, our new heart leads us into the counsel of God as we submit to its direction. Yes, our new heart has a brain, and that brain is the mind of Christ.

The old heart can function independently of the brain. The new heart also has this ability, but even more so—because it is *supernatural*. The old (natural) "nerve" connection has been severed, so this heart is able to rule your old brain because it was not with your original body at conception. It was never oversaturated with information by your old brain, so it has the power to take authority. This heart has not been naturally conditioned to bow to your mind through years of familiarity. Your new heart has the undeniable ability to walk in the statues of God.

When you say, "I have been born again in Christ Jesus," the first thing that begins to function and rule in that space is the heart.

Your new heart has the undeniable ability to walk in the statutes of God.

And I will give them one heart [a new heart] and I will put a new spirit within them; and I will take the stony [unnaturally hardened] heart out of their flesh, and will give them a heart of flesh [sensitive and responsive to the touch of their God]. That they may walk in My statutes and keep My ordinances, and do them. And they shall be My people, and I will be their God.
—EZEKIEL 11:19–20

It is incredible to me that God has allowed scientists to prove (to Christians) the difference between a person that says, "I have been touched," and somebody that has truly been converted. When you have been converted *for real*, you receive a new heart, and that heart takes you back to the beginning—to when you were a fetus—because your new heart beats without being connected to the brain, just like in the unborn child.

Nicodemus, a ruler of the Pharisees and one of the wisest men of his day, was stumped by the mystery of the new birth.

Jesus answered him, I assure you, most solemnly I tell you, that unless a person is born again (anew, from above), he cannot ever see (know, be acquainted with, and experience) the kingdom of God. Nicodemus said to Him, How can a man be born when he is old? Can he enter his mother's womb again and be born? Jesus answered, I assure you, most solemnly I tell you, unless a man is born of water and [even] the Spirit, he cannot [ever] enter the kingdom of God. What is born of [from] the flesh is flesh [of the physical is physical]; and what is born of the Spirit is spirit...If I have told you of things that happen right here on the earth and yet none of you believes Me, how can you believe (trust Me, adhere to Me, rely on Me) if I tell you of heavenly things? And yet no one has ever gone up to heaven, but there is One Who has come down from heaven—the Son of Man [Himself], Who is (dwells, has His home) in heaven.

—JOHN 3:3–6, 12–13

Nicodemus had earthly wisdom, not the wisdom of God. If we are to embrace the new heart, we must receive and believe the Word of the Lord.

More on the Anatomy of the Heart

By the twenty-fifth day of a woman's pregnancy, the heart has formed and started its rhythm. Outside of any legal definition, some doctors say that death really occurs when the heart stops beating, because the heart is alive before the brain is formed and can continue beating after the brain is dead.

Through its beating patterns, the heart sends pressure waves that move through our arteries to create our pulse rhythms. Heartbeats also influence brainwave activity and provide oxygen, nutrients and electrical energy to every organ and gland in our bodies.

Researchers have documented that when a pulse of blood gets up to the brain, it changes the brain's electrical activity. It alters the flow of that brain's process! Your new heart is also able to send "waves" of life, quickening your brain and the rest of your being to the ways of God.

> But if the Spirit of him that raised up Jesus from the dead dwell in you, he that raised up Christ from the dead shall also quicken your mortal bodies by his Spirit that dwelleth in you. Therefore, brethren, we are debtors, not to the flesh, to live after the flesh. For if ye live after the flesh, ye shall die: but if ye through the Spirit do mortify the deeds of the body, ye shall live.
> —ROMANS 8:11–13, KJV

Of the trillions of cells in the human body, heart cells are the only ones that can pulsate. With every pulsation, "intelligent communication" takes place. According to cardio-energetics (a newer field of science), our heart *mediates* our thoughts, feelings, fears and dreams. It also keeps our bodies in chemical balance. (See "the balance hormone" in chapter six.) Research has also revealed that the heart has a powerful impact outside of the body as well. For example, when nurses played a recorded heartbeat in a hospital nursery, the crying was reduced by almost 55 percent. The beats become their rhythm—an emotional "life support" system.[1]

Unlike the brain, or any other organ in the body, we can feel, hear and sense our hearts. Our heart not only affects every cell in our bodies, its electromagnetic field also has been measured to radiate outside of the body, even up to ten feet away.[2] Any way you look at it, the heart is magnetic.

The Atmosphere of the New Heart

God tells us that He has a pattern for us to follow that will keep our new hearts alive. It is an atmosphere where our new hearts will thrive. It restores everything to a state of balance and harmony with God. It is the atmosphere of worship.

> Therefore also now, says the Lord, turn and keep on coming to Me with all your heart, with fasting, with weeping, and with mourning [until every hindrance is removed and the broken fellowship is restored]. Rend your hearts and not your garments and return to the Lord, your God, for He is gracious and merciful, slow to anger, and abounding in loving-kindness; and He revokes His sentence of evil [when His conditions are met].
>
> —JOEL 2:12–13

There is another amazing fact about the beating heart that ties into this. If you place several heart cells together (but not touching) in a dish, with no nerve cell connecting them, they will fall into the same beating pattern, one that is different from the beat of each individual cell.

This is the same balancing principle that I mentioned in chapter seven, only greater. The "clock" balance represented everything in your body aligning with your heart—since the heart has the most energy. This "heart cell" balance ties the heart to its Creator.

God desires that we dedicate ourselves fully to Him, trusting in and obeying His instructions. As we do this, our new hearts are strengthened, and an atmosphere of righteousness, worship and purification is created that reminds your heart of its heavenly home.

> Therefore say to them [the Jews of this day], Thus says the Lord of hosts: Return to Me, says the Lord of hosts, and I will return to you; it is the utterance of the Lord of hosts…I appeal to you therefore, brethren, and beg of you in view of [all] the mercies of God, to make a decisive dedication of your bodies [presenting all your members and faculties] as a living sacrifice, holy (devoted, consecrated) and well pleasing to God, which is your reasonable (rational, intelligent) service and spiritual worship.
> —ZECHARIAH 1:3; ROMANS 12:1

Your new heart comes from a purified place, so in order for it to be strong enough to stay in a willing position, you have to keep it in this type of atmosphere.

When a baby is delivered out of its mother's womb, the nurses wrap the baby up and hand it to the mother, who holds her baby close to her heart. This makes the newborn feel warm and protected, just like when that baby lived in the womb.

If you take a fish out of the ocean, it can survive as

long as you put it back in water within a short period of time. You cannot take a fish out of the ocean, its place of origin where it survives and thrives, bring it home and lay it on your living room table. It will never live like that. If you take it from water where it is accustomed to living, you have to put it back into water in order for it to stay alive.

Your new heart comes from the Spirit realm, so you have to keep it in the atmosphere of the Spirit in order for it to exist.

A baby fights to stay in the womb, and a fish will fight when you take it out of the water. It is the same with the new heart. It "hungers and thirsts" after righteousness—it will suffocate if you take it out of God's presence. If you have a new heart, you should get to the point that you cannot get enough of God, church or God's people—because this heart lives and thrives in the atmosphere of worship.

Your new heart desires the things of God above the things of this world. You will find yourself saying, "I have to wash dishes, but I feel like glorifying God!" No longer will you have the thought ringing in your heart, *Oh no, I have to pray*, or *I have to go to church*, or *I have to worship*. Instead, as you prepare to go about your daily duties, getting ready for work, you will think, *I have to go to work, but I want to stay here in His presence!*

Your new heart will no longer sit in your pew at church and have to be forced to worship! No longer will you watch the clock as you hurriedly take three minutes to pray as your day begins. No longer will you have to deal with feelings of dislike or hatred toward your fellow man. Your new heart will compel you to love others.

This heart is bursting with the characteristics of Christ and longs for opportunities to express Christ through your actions. Because it "hungers and thirsts" for God, you must nourish it and feed it through your "Christ-life" living. Your new heart comes from the Spirit realm, so you have to keep it in the atmosphere of the Spirit in order for it to exist.

The new heart comes from glory—from God Himself, from heaven—where the heavenly host worships and praises Him continually. His glory, purification, righteousness and awesome presence surrounded your heart like a warm blanket before He gave it to you. This heart cannot rest in the midst of junk. You have to put it in the same atmosphere that it was birthed out of.

> My son, attend to my words; consent and submit to my sayings. Let them not depart from your sight; keep them in the center of your heart. For they are life to those who find them, healing and health to all their flesh. Keep and guard your heart with all vigilance and above all that you guard, for out of it flow the springs of life.
>
> —PROVERBS 4:20–23

Responding to the Rhythms
of the New Heart

There is another amazing thing about your heartbeat: It responds to music. Just as the heart influences the *autonomic* (subconscious, automatic)
functions of your body (like breathing, for example),
the new heart will gently begin to influence your
behavior. You will desire to do something that will
please God, sometimes even before you have learned
the scripture that tells you that is what you should
do! (See 1 Thessalonians 4:1.)

I have seen people who were converted who did not
know the first thing about God before their conversion. They had not been raised in the church, yet they
had an experience with God. After their conversion
they started saying things like, "He told me to turn
that movie off." "He told me to take those clothes off
and not to wear that because it was too seductive."
"He told me to take the earring out of my lip."

Sometimes I would ask, "You found that in the
Scriptures?"

They would reply, "No, I have not read about it, but
that is what God told me to do." They began to
respond automatically to the new information flowing out of their new hearts. In Galatians 5:16 we read:

> But I say, walk and live [habitually] in the
> [Holy] Spirit [responsive to and controlled and
> guided by the Spirit]; then you will certainly
> not gratify the cravings and desires of the flesh
> (of human nature without God).

This verse refers to the fact that you have been *disconnected* from your brain because you are no longer responding to its demands. You are obeying the gentle promptings of Almighty God! Because of that, you no longer follow the carnal, fleshly prompting of the flesh. Verses 17–21 describe those fleshly desires:

> For the desires of the flesh are opposed to the [Holy] Spirit, and the [desires of the] Spirit are opposed to the flesh (godless human nature); for these are antagonistic to each other [continually withstanding and in conflict with each other], so that you are not free, but are prevented from doing what you desire to do. But if you are guided (led) by the [Holy] Spirit, you are not subject to the Law. Now the doings (practices) of the flesh are clear (obvious): they are immorality, impurity, indecency, idolatry, sorcery, enmity, strife, jealousy, anger (ill-temper), selfishness, divisions (dissensions), party spirit (factions, sects with peculiar opinions, heresies), envy, drunkenness, carousing, and the like. I warn you beforehand…that those who do such things shall not inherit the kingdom of God.

Do not be like a fish out of water. God does not want you to die! Submit to the ways of God, and your new heart will thrive, bringing life to every other part of your being. Verses 22–24 continue by describing the life your new heart brings to you:

> But the fruit of the [Holy] Spirit [the work which His presence within accomplishes] is love, joy (gladness), peace, patience (an even temper, forbearance), kindness, goodness

(benevolence), faithfulness, gentleness (meek-
ness, humility), self-control (self-restraint, con-
tinence). Against such things there is no law
[that can bring a charge]. And those who
belong to Christ Jesus (the Messiah) have crucified the flesh (the godless human nature) with
its passions and appetites and desires.

If we live by the Holy Spirit, how do we crucify the
flesh with our new heart?

If we live by the [Holy] Spirit, let us also walk
by the Spirit. [If by the Holy Spirit we have our
life in God, let us go forward walking in line, our
conduct controlled by the Spirit.] Let us not
become vainglorious and self-conceited, competitive and challenging and provoking and irri-
tating to one another, envying and being jealous
of one another.

—GALATIANS 5:25–26

All of these things have been described by *scientists* (not by the church) as being the workings of the
mind! Because this is a competitive world, and our
old brains have been trained (according to medical
doctors) to *compete*, Christians have become "…
self-conceited, competitive…challenging…jealous
of one another."

Our minds are determined to stay on top, be
number one over our hearts and bodies. So our
minds have learned to keep gathering more and
more information. The old mind tries to run the old
heart into the ground as your brain attempts to keep
up with the latest information, technology and
everything else, just to stay competitive.

When this happens inside of you, when you

become aware of the fact that you are jealous of people and competitive, it is time to make a change.
Something is wrong if you are having these kinds of
thoughts: *Do I preach better than this person? Who
sings the best? Whose church is larger?* Such
thoughts are the workings of your mind. They do not
flow from the heart of God.

Across this nation, the church must become aware
of her need to crucify the flesh with our new hearts.
The church has not yet tapped into the heart of God.
In too many instances, our brains are leading us.

It has been scientifically proven that when people
undergo lobotomies, a procedure where part of the
brain is removed, they can still survive. *Yet you cannot remove a person's heart and expect that person
to live.* The same is true of our new hearts. Your life
is hidden in God, which is the essence of your new
heart. You cannot remove the new heart and expect
to live spiritually.

Another interesting fact about the brain is that it
has no feeling. If we apply this spiritually, we can discover why people can curse you out and not feel it.
They can do evil things and think evil thoughts, and
not be spiritually aware or pained by their actions.
The reason is because they have cut off the intelligent language of their new heart. The Scriptures tell
us repeatedly to "hearken" unto the word of the
Lord. (See Leviticus 26; Deuteronomy 15:5; 1 Kings
11:38; Proverbs 8:32; Isaiah 46:12.) In the Hebrew,
this word *hearken* means "to hear intelligently."[3]

The brain, on the other hand, has so much information coming into it, that it overloads and paralyzes
the old heart. The old heart could not compete

against it. This is one of the main reasons why your new heart has to be disconnected from the mind. Your new heart has come loaded with divine information that has not yet been revealed to man! So it always tells that old brain, "I know stuff that you do not know. I know things that your intellect could never comprehend! The only way you will ever be able to understand is if God reveals it to you!"

Only the Blood Can Save Us

There is another, even more amazing thing about the new heart, old mind disconnection. Since the arteries, which transport the blood, are no longer connected by nerve endings to the old heart, they establish the connection to our new hearts. Praise God! Only by the blood can the heart rule the mind. The blood is how the new heart stays purified, because it is continuously cycled through the heart on its way to the rest of the body. The blood of Jesus can literally "wash away your sin," making you "white as snow" (pure) in His sight!

There is life in the blood! So when Jesus said, "You are cleansed and pruned already, because of the word which I have given you," He was revealing a spiritual process (John 15:3). The Word enters the mind and cleanses it; then the blood flows through and gives it life. The Word of God is alive because Jesus shed His blood and transformed typed pages into a living reality! His blood brings the Word alive. It makes the gospel work.

Even more than this, just as a heart transplant

patient must receive life-giving blood transfusions as a part of the transplant process, so when you receive a new heart, you have also received *new blood*—Christ's blood!

This new blood identifies you with the Father and sets the atmosphere for the new heart. It cleanses you as it fills every part of your being with the character of Christ. That character (which defines who you are) is passed to you through your heavenly Father's DNA. Jesus was the identical image of God because He diligently followed His new heart. He said, "Anyone who has seen Me has seen the Father" (John 14:9).

For this reason we must be "born again" and receive the new heart. The spiritual DNA in our new blood is eternally new. It makes us "sons" and "daughters" of God, causing us to look more like Him as we obey our new heart. DNA always reveals who the real father is!

The Heart Cry of God

Understand [this], my beloved brethren. Let every man be quick to hear [a ready listener], slow to speak, slow to take offense and to get angry. For man's anger does not promote the righteousness God [wishes and requires]. So get rid of all uncleanness and the rampant outgrowth of wickedness, and in a humble (gentle, modest) spirit receive and welcome the Word which implanted and rooted [in your hearts] contains the power to save your souls.

—JAMES 1:19–21

Your new heart is the heart of God. It comes with His will, His ways, His purpose, assignment and obedience already in it! This heart, and *only* this heart, contains the *power* to change the way you live.

So ask yourself these questions: "Am I really saved? Though I cried on the altar, did I really get converted? Though I am in church, faithful to attend services...I sit on the second pew every Sunday...has my heart been changed? Did I really receive a heart transplant from God?"

Do I really have the new heart?

Chapter 9

The Renewed **Mind**

I f you have received the new heart, chances are you remember when it happened. Suddenly your responses to the world began to change— sometimes to your own surprise. The spiritual transformation begins to manifest itself in your physical body. To do so, it must be processed through your brain.

When God gives you a new heart, it is the deposit, or assurance, from God that He is also going to make your mind new. The old (natural) brain is formed, step by step, into four different sections. Although you get a whole new heart at once, the mind must be transformed in stages and in levels. Going back to conception, the heart forms and beats before the brain is created. Then it grows from the bottom up, starting with the medulla, amygdala, cerebral cortex and finally the frontal lobes. According to medicine, the heart transplant is immediate, but the mind transformation is progressive.

The Four Stages of Mind Transformation

For Christians, our daily battleground is the progressive state of renewing our minds.

> Therefore, my dear ones, as you have always obeyed [my suggestions], so now, not only [with the enthusiasm you would show] in my presence but much more because I am absent, work out (cultivate, carry out to the goal, and fully complete) your own salvation with reverence and awe and trembling (self-distrust, with serious caution, tenderness of conscience, watchfulness against temptation, timidly shrinking from whatever might offend God and discredit the name of Christ). [Not in your own strength] for it is God Who is all the while effectually at work in you [energizing and creating in you the power and desire], both to will and to work for His good pleasure and satisfaction and delight.
>
> —PHILIPPIANS 2:12–13

As you submit to God through your new heart, He balances your entire being. Your body starts to pulse with the new rhythms from your new heart, blood pressure waves hit your brain, and the old mind begins to respond to the new flow of your heart. And although the immediate effect may be subtle, you discover that you no longer think the same way anymore. Subtly, but consistently, the way you think and the way you do things change.

Let us briefly review the development of the mind as we learned in chapter six. The mind begins to develop after the heart is already in place, and it grows from the bottom up. The *medulla oblongata* establishes the link between the automatic functions of the heart, mind and body. Then the *amygdala* develops, which stores emotional memories and forms the basis of your perceptions. Out of the amygdala, the *logic* centers form, beginning with the cerebral cortex, where complex thought patterns like planning, strategizing, reflection, inspiration and imagination emerge. Lastly, the *frontal lobes* develop, allowing you to make decisions based on emotional and logical input. This section feeds back into the amygdala, telling it how to react or respond from the emotional memories.[1]

According to medicine, the heart transplant is immediate, but the mind transformation is progressive.

Each stage of your mind's development must be renewed. The Word must "pierce" each part of the mind, transforming thought and emotion on the sub-conscious and conscious levels.

The Four Levels of Consciousness

Just as there are four sections of the brain, there are four levels of consciousness called *brainwaves*, or electrical currents that cycle through it. We know them as *Beta, Alpha, Theta* and *Delta*. They are measured by the power of the impulse, or frequency, as well as speed, which determines the category. Beta cycles through your brain eighteen to thirty times per second; Alpha is next at eight to twelve cycles, followed by Theta at four to seven cycles, and finally to Delta waves at less than six cycles per second. The faster the cycles, the higher your level of consciousness will be.[2]

Most people function on the Beta level while they are awake. This level is fast, but not the most efficient. The logic and problem solving of the frontal lobes and cerebral cortex are easiest in Beta; however, your thoughts often "collide" on this level. Researchers say that you cannot stop or slow Beta waves down long enough to focus on just one thought, causing you to miss important details. This is how the old mind deceives you. Logic and decision making, which require crystal-clear thinking, cannot be clear and focused when your heart and mind are out of balance.

Americans live in an instant society, so Beta thinking is very welcome here. We want things to happen fast, so we take things into our own hands. God is not pleased. Beta thoughts wear and tear on your heart (and your entire body) if you remain on this level too long. Yet the "ruling" brain loves Beta; it will keep you from slowing down and listening to your heart whenever it can. Like stress, Beta thinking can be a silent killer. Before you realize it, your thought patterns are in overdrive, and breakdown is imminent.

Alpha bridges your conscious and subconscious minds. It has been called the most productive cycle, and it was the first that people learned to identify

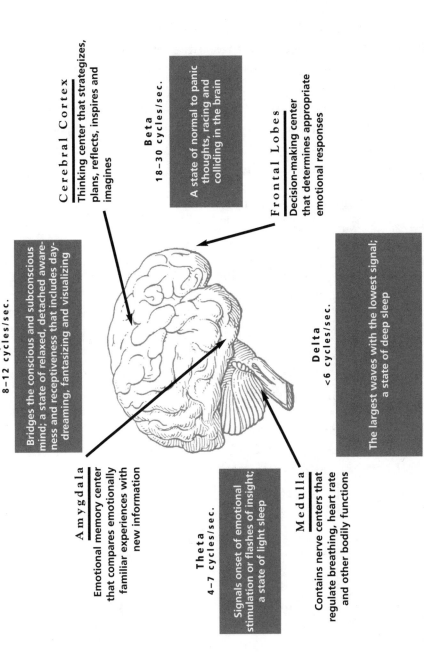

Cerebral Cortex
Thinking center that strategizes, plans, reflects, inspires and imagines

Beta
18-30 cycles/sec.
A state of normal to panic thoughts, racing and colliding in the brain

Frontal Lobes
Decision-making center that determines appropriate emotional responses

Alpha
8-12 cycles/sec.
Bridges the conscious and subconscious mind; a state of relaxed, detached awareness and receptiveness that includes daydreaming, fantasizing and visualizing

Delta
<6 cycles/sec.
The largest waves with the lowest signal; a state of deep sleep

Amygdala
Emotional memory center that compares emotionally familiar experiences with new information

Theta
4-7 cycles/sec.
Signals onset of emotional stimulation or flashes of insight; a state of light sleep

Medulla
Contains nerve centers that regulate breathing, heart rate and other bodily functions

Adapted from Childre and Martin, *The HeartMath Solution*, 31, Figure 2.2, "Neurological Communication from the Heart to the Brain."

and control. Alpha is an alert, daydreaming state, a relaxed, detached awareness that reflects a receptive mind. Alpha seems to function primarily between the cerebral cortex and the amygdala. If Alpha is lost, the link to your subconscious mind is broken. You will not be able to remember details about your dreams or visions from God. Alpha is the link between "knowing" and "doing."

> Stand in awe, and sin not: commune with your own heart upon your bed, and be still.
>
> —PSALM 4:4, KJV

The Alpha state is where you have chosen to "be still" and know that God is in control (Ps. 46:10). It is the *meditative* state, where you are aware of your surroundings, but more tuned into your inner consciousness. Problem solving becomes easier, and your intuitions run deeper. You catch the thoughts that are missed in Beta.

Many have been hurt, bruised and offended because their minds— *not* their hearts—were leading them.

Theta is the next level, occurring while you are in a light sleep. Theta waves are slower than Alpha waves, but more intense, usually indicating emotional stimulation. They are linked with childlike thoughts and insecurities (children up to the age of puberty have high readings of Theta waves).[3] Theta waves seem to operate hand in hand with amygdala thinking, and they can also tap into deeper thought patterns. Flash insights come from the Theta realm. For example, have you ever thought, *Something is not right here...I do not know what it is, but something is wrong.*

Sometimes Theta brainwaves relate to those *gut feelings* we all have from time to time. Have you ever thought, *Do not go that way*, but you went anyway? Then something happened that could have been avoided. Most likely, your new heart was connecting with Theta brainwaves. So many times when something goes wrong, we think back on the incident and say, "I had a gut feeling!" In reality, our heart was forewarning us of danger—already having perceived what was going to happen—but we were not in the right state of consciousness to receive the full revelation. We cannot speed around in Beta thinking and expect to have new heart insight. Many have been hurt, bruised and offended because their minds—*not* their hearts—were leading them.

Delta thinking is where "deep calleth unto deep" —the subconscious mind—where "all thy waves and thy billows are gone over me" (Ps. 42:7, KJV). This is the abyss, the deepest depth of your mind; you cannot measure, understand or control it. This is where God can change your temperament and behavior without you even knowing it! There is a saying: "A leopard can't change its spots." It can, and it will, if the Word of God is allowed to pierce on the Delta level.

Delta is where your mind can receive the "meat" of the Word as it pierces to the depths of your innermost being—where Delta and Theta waves unite. Like a child, you embrace the truth and trust God with a deep, calm awareness. David said, "Even at night my heart instructs me" (Ps. 16:7, NIV). On the Delta thought level, "all things are possible with God" (Mark 10:27). This deep, subconscious transformation flows up—through your emotions and logic—to illuminate your entire being. When the new heart is in complete control, electric impulses are *supernatural*—because the natural link has been cut. This mind is controlled by the power of God!

The Emotional Mind

As you have read, *conscious thought* begins and ends in your emotions. Emotions give meaning to facts generated by your logic—that is why our logical centers grow out of our emotions. The word *emotion* literally means "energy in motion." It is a strong feeling—like love, anger, joy or sorrow—that moves us. Basically, emotional energy is neutral. It is our logical thoughts and physical reactions that make our emotions either positive or negative.

People tend to think that emotions come from the heart. The truth is that both our mind and heart drive them.

Head emotions are self-centered and defensive. They are moved by "what you can do for me." They want instant gratification. They are like conditional love, which says, "I'll love you, if you love me and meet my needs." Brain emotions will *drive* you to do things that are unwise or dangerous.

Heart emotions run deeper and are selfless. They express themselves without expecting anything in return. Heart emotions reflect emotional maturity; they are balanced and offer solutions to problems rather than participating in them. They are like *agape* love, which is the love God shows to us. God, who understands our weaknesses, sees the problems we bring upon ourselves and helps us find solutions, yet He does not become entangled in our problems. He loves us in spite of ourselves, and He expects nothing from us in return.

Circumcision of the Heart

Because God understands us so thoroughly, He has chosen to rule in our lives through our new heart. When He established a covenant relationship with Israel (through Moses), He did it through circumcision—a cutting of the flesh, which drew blood. When God began to teach us the spiritual implications behind this physical act of circumcision, He taught us about the circumcision of the heart.

God could not establish a covenant relationship with us through the brain. The brain says, "I will do something for you only if you will do something for me." The love and obedience that flow from our brains are conditional—dependent upon "what's in it for me!"

But the new heart says, "I will love you...obey you...care for you even if you will not respond to me. I will, in spite of what I see from you. I will, regardless of the way you treat me...I am still able to love you." The church has not yet been perfected in love, because the minute we are offended by people, we stop loving them. The minute we see something in our church, or in our pastor, that we do not like, we leave the church. Our brains are leading us.

The brain gathers all of the facts, information and emotions. Then it rationalizes or reasons them out. When it gets through calculating, it says, "I like you, for now." The new heart (which comes from our Father) looks at everything, but because it is eternal, it sees beyond who a person is now to what he is going to become—and loves him until he gets there. This can only be done when you are equipped with knowledge that is beyond this earth. Believers should not see things as "natural" people do. We should see things as God sees them, because we are looking through the eyes of our new heart.

Without the governing influence of the new heart, we can fall prey to negative emotions like fear, anger, blame or insecurity. When this heart comes into a person's body, that person begins to see with a new perspective, even if he or she does not understand why. When we have a new heart, we learn to respond instead of react. For example, if someone offends you, the *natural* reaction would be anger because the emotion would be charged by the natural thought pattern. But a mind that has been renewed according to the Word can look at an offense and call it a blessing. The renewed mind is powerful.

Sometimes when a person is in the physical healing process, a doctor will say, "She's fighting…" The person may have been wounded by a gunshot and may have all the probable signs indicating death. Yet in spite of the injury, the doctor says, "...but she's fighting." That person's mind is saying, "I know that I am shot. I know that I am bleeding to death, but I am fighting to live." Very often it is the mind's response to an incident that determines the outcome.

The same is true spiritually. When the heart and brain are out of alignment (resulting in an unrenewed mind), the thought patterns that are released into the world by way of the flesh will always be negative. This deceptive thinking can mean the difference between life and death.

Your new heart reveals the truth. Its substance is Truth, so it reveals the truth. That is why we can look at something that Satan has camouflaged to look like God and call it a lie. We are also able to look at something that has the "form of godliness" and know that it denies the "power thereof." Why? There is no truth in it. Why? Eternal love does not live there. Jesus said, "And you will know the Truth, and the Truth will set you free" (John 8:32).

Why Didn't I Think?

Scientists have observed that *feeling* is faster than *thought*, so our emotional reactions show up in brain activity before we have time to think. As soon as we perceive something, our emotions are active. We think, or process the perception, afterward. This is the reason we say things before we realize why we have said them. Emotions, even though they are influenced by our thoughts, *act* much faster. Doctors have concluded that we cannot manage our emotions through our rational mind. We react, and then we think.

Remember the four sections of the mind—the medulla (breathing, heart rate and other body functions), the amygdala (storehouse of emotional memory), the cerebral cortex (plans, strategies, reflection, inspiration and imagination) and the frontal lobes (decision making). The heart pumps blood through the medulla to the amygdala and changes its electrical activity. This confirms that our emotions move faster than our logic centers, or the slow brainwave patterns associated with our subconscious mind. Our brains cannot manage our emotions—and transform our lives—without the heart's regulating influence.

Unless we receive the new heart, we will always react through our amygdala via the old, evil heart. So I may blow your brains out and then later think with my logic, *I should not have done that.* You could slap somebody because your old heart runs offensive information straight to your emotion center. If you have an old heart (which is of Satan), and you cuss somebody out, the amygdala may get you slapped! Later (*always* later) the logical centers would say, "I should have thought first. I should have gone for a walk. I should not have slapped her. Then I would not have lost my job."

When you have received a heart transplant from God, your first response from the amygdala should be what God would do. Upon seeing your response, a person operating from the cerebral cortex, frontal lobes area of his or her mind would ask, "Why didn't you slap her? Why didn't you cuss her out?"

Standing there (with the heart of God) you would say, "I could not open my mouth. The Holy Spirit would not let me say a word."

A cerebral, frontal person would ask, "Why did you give her a ride [when it is raining] when you know she cannot stand you?"

You would respond, "The Holy Spirit told me to stop my car and let her get in."

When you get home, your mind would say, "I do not even know why I did that, because I know that she does not like me."

Scientific study has proven that the emotions get messages directly from the heart. This means the first response you see will reveal the nature of a person's heart.

I know this is true from my own experiences. God has put me in predicaments where I *knew* I should have gone off about something, yet He would not let me open my mouth. I *knew* that I had been wronged, but God still led me to bless the people who wronged me. Now I understand, from my fresh understanding of science, how God makes this happen. It is not easy for the flesh, but the more you submit to your new heart, the easier it will become.

Unraveling the Mystery of the Mind

Since the new heart is no longer connected to the brain by the nerves, it can control every part of the mind with its power—its pulsating authority. This is how a new heart can take up residence in a person's body and *cause* the mind to do *strange* things. The old mind has begun to be controlled by the power of the new heart and is *no longer* controlled by the limited power of the nerve endings. Nerve endings can only release measured amounts of power at a time to that brain. When the new heart controls the brain with its pulsating power, it can send spiritual power as strong as is needed in order to change that mind.

> For with the heart a person believes (adheres to, trusts in, and relies on Christ) and so is justified (declared righteous, acceptable to God), and with the mouth he confesses (declares openly and speaks out freely his faith) and confirms [his] salvation.
>
> —ROMANS 10:10

Your new heart is already equipped with the ability to believe God. It comes "built with faith." The mind must learn to demonstrate, on every level, what the heart believes. A powerful confidence flows out of the new heart, a confidence Jesus demonstrated when He came into the world.

Jesus said confidently, "I am the door...I am the way...I am the resurrection." He did not say, "I *think* I am the door...I *think* I am the way...I *think* I am the resurrection." And if Jesus Christ, indeed, is the Word "made flesh" that has dwelled among us—and now the Word lives inside of us—we can now make the same confessions. Confidently we can declare, "I am healed; I am delivered; I am set free!" If I believe "unto salvation," then this is how I am able to say that I am saved. God knows when He is alive and well inside of us.

The Bible says, "Out of the abundance of the heart the mouth speaketh" (Matt. 12:34, KJV). Whatever your heart is full of…whatever overflows from it…is what your mouth is going to speak. When you say, "I am saved," it is because your heart is full, overflowing with abundance and salvation.

The Mind/Body Connection

The second chapter of 1 Corinthians gives an awesome understanding of the mind/body connection. Let's take a close look at what the Word is teaching us in this chapter.

The apostle Paul was a highly educated man in traditional religion. Yet as he begins this chapter, he clearly states that he was determined that his new heart would not be reconnected to his philosophy or to anything that he had studied in the past. He opted for a permanent disconnection!

> As for myself, brethren, when I came to you, I did not come proclaiming to you the testimony and evidence or mystery and secret of God [concerning what He has done through Christ for the salvation of men] in lofty words of eloquence or human philosophy and wisdom. For I resolve to know nothing (to be acquainted with nothing, to make a display of the knowledge of nothing, and to be conscious of nothing) among you except Jesus Christ (the Messiah) and Him crucified.
>
> —1 CORINTHIANS 2:1–2

In verses 3–7 he teaches us about *heart wisdom*—something very different from the knowledge from the mind. It was a wisdom available only to those who have received a new heart. Paul describes this experience by saying:

> And I was in (passed into a state of) weakness and fear (dread) and great trembling [after I had come] among you. And my language and my message were not set forth in persuasive (enticing and plausible) words of wisdom, but they were in demonstration of the [Holy] Spirit and power [a proof by the Spirit and power of God, operating on me and stirring in the minds of my hearers the most holy emotions and thus persuading them], so that your faith might not rest in the wisdom of men (human philosophy), but in the power of God. Yet when we are among the full-grown (spiritually mature Christians who are ripe in understanding), we do impart a [higher] wisdom (the knowledge of the divine plan previously hidden); but it is indeed not a wisdom of this present age or of this world nor of the leaders and rulers of this age, who are being brought to nothing and are doomed to pass away. But rather what we are setting forth is a wisdom of God once hidden [from the human understanding] and now revealed to us by God—[that wisdom] which God devised and decreed before the ages for our glorification [to lift us into the glory of His presence].

Paul stated, "None of the rulers of this age or world perceived and recognized and understood this, for if they had, they would never have crucified the Lord of glory" (v. 8). Why did he say this? Because by crucifying Christ, the Lord of glory, they gave Jesus the power to live inside of us. This enabled people to receive divine wisdom and revelation from the "new heart"—things that had not yet been revealed to

man. This new heart wisdom would eventually out-
run them and supersede the mind knowledge upon
which they based their whole lives. It would expose
them and bring glory to Christ—the very glory they
tried to destroy.

Through Paul, God is teaching us that we cannot
grab hold of God—or of the knowledge and wisdom
that is God's alone—with our natural minds. To understand God we must receive the new heart. In Joel 2:13
God tells us the only way to receive this new heart. We
must "rend [our] hearts and not [our] garments and
return to the Lord."

In verses 9–11 of 1 Corinthians 2, Paul points out
the utter futility of trying to grab hold of God in any
other way:

> But, on the contrary, as the Scripture says,
> What eye has not seen and ear has not heard
> and has not entered into the heart of man, [all
> that] God has prepared (made and keeps ready)
> for those who love Him [who hold Him in affec-
> tionate reverence, promptly obeying Him and
> gratefully recognizing the benefits He has
> bestowed]. Yet to us God has unveiled and
> revealed them by and through His Spirit, for the
> [Holy] Spirit searches diligently, exploring and
> examining everything, even sounding the pro-
> found and bottomless things of God [the divine
> counsels and things hidden and beyond man's
> scrutiny]. For what person perceives (knows
> and understands) what passes through a man's
> thoughts except the man's own spirit within
> him? Just so no one discerns (comes to know
> and comprehend) the thoughts of God except
> the Spirit of God.

Paul continues by explaining the role of the Holy Spirit in receiving our new heart:

> Now we have not received the spirit [that belongs to] the world, but the [Holy] Spirit Who is from God, [given to us] that we might realize and comprehend and appreciate the gifts [of divine favor and blessing so freely and lavishly] bestowed on us by God. And we are setting these truths forth in words not taught by human wisdom but taught by the [Holy] Spirit, combining and interpreting spiritual truths with spiritual language [to those who possess the Holy Spirit].
>
> —1 CORINTHIANS 2:12–13

This heart wisdom that comes from our new heart is available only to those who possess the Holy Spirit. The Holy Spirit does not baptize our mind! We receive the baptism of the Holy Spirit in our hearts, and when this happens, God teaches and trains us how to combine the spiritual "deposit" with the new, spiritual language.

> But the natural, nonspiritual man does not accept or welcome or admit into his heart the gifts and teachings and revelations of the Spirit of God, for they are folly (meaningless nonsense) to him; and he is incapable of knowing them (of progressively recognizing, understanding, and becoming better acquainted with them) because they are spiritually discerned and estimated and appreciated. But the spiritual man tries all things [he examines, investigates, inquires into, questions, and discerns all things], yet is himself to be put on trial and judged by no one [he can read the meaning of everything, but no one can properly discern

or appraise or get an insight into him]. For who
has known or understood the mind (the coun-
sels and purposes) of the Lord so as to guide
and instruct Him and give Him knowledge? But
we have the mind of Christ (the Messiah) and
do hold the thoughts (feelings and purposes) of
His heart.

—1 Corinthians 2:14–16, emphasis added

The mind of Christ is the mind of the Word! God has
given us the Bible literally to "possess" His mind—the
mind of Christ—the Word made flesh. Once we possess His mind, we "do hold the thoughts (feelings
[emotions!] and purposes) of His heart" (v. 16).

Evidence That We Have a New Heart

Paul helps us to recognize the evidence that we have
received a new heart and possess the heart wisdom
about which he is speaking in 1 Corinthians 2. A
newborn infant cannot understand the intelligent
language of his adult parents, but must learn to
speak as he grows. So too a spiritual "infant" in
Christ must learn a "spiritual language." Paul continues:

However, brethren, I could not talk to you as to
spiritual [men], but as to nonspiritual [men of
the flesh, in whom the carnal nature predomi-
nates], as to mere infants [in the new life] in
Christ [unable to talk yet!]

—1 Corinthians 3:1

Paul was not speaking about using sentences or

words in a natural language. He was indicating that these new believers were unable to talk "spiritual language." He continued by saying:

> I fed you with milk, not solid food, for you were not yet strong enough [to be ready for it]; but even yet you are not strong enough [to be ready for it], for you are still [unspiritual, having the nature] of the flesh [under the control of ordinary impulses]. For as long as [there are] envying and jealousy and wrangling and factions among you, are you not unspiritual and of the flesh, behaving yourselves after a human standard and like mere (unchanged) men?
>
> —1 CORINTHIANS 3:2–3

Paul was saying that these new believers were still controlled by "ordinary impulses," the nerve endings leading to and coming from the old heart. They adopted "human standards" because they did not have the new heart. A few verses later, Paul warned these spiritual "infants" to be prepared to be tested.

> But if anyone builds upon the Foundation, whether it be with gold, silver, precious stones, wood, hay, straw, the work of each [one] will become [plainly, openly] known (shown for what it is); for the day [of Christ] will disclose and declare it, because it will be revealed with fire, and the fire will test and critically appraise the character and worth of the work each person has done.
>
> —1 CORINTHIANS 3:12–13

We need to heed these words from Paul. It's foolish to go around "thinking" you have a new heart when indeed you have not yet received it. As the old adage says, "Don't talk the talk until you can walk the walk!" A day of testing is coming, and when you get in the fire, when it is time to be tested to see what you are made of—the fire is going to reveal your work. The fire will reveal whether your heart is made of gold, silver and precious stones (the new heart) or if it is composed of hay, wood, stubble or straw (the old heart). The fire of walking in what you believe and the fire of being tested come to "appraise" your character, to see of what you are made.

We will be tested in the fire of our daily living. The enemy will throw his fiery darts at us. But the fire does not come to harm us—it comes to appraise us. It is in the crucible of God's fire of testing that the evidence of our new heart begins to shine forth. It is as though God is saying, "Just checking. Just checking to see if My heart is still in there. Just checking to see if My blood is still running through your veins."

> The fire of walking in what you believe and the fire of being tested come to "appraise" your character, to see of what you are made.

The test of fire allows the new heart to shine forth. For those who pass the test and reveal the new heart, there will be a reward.

If the work which any person has built on this Foundation [any product of His efforts whatever] survives [this test], he will get his reward.

—1 CORINTHIANS 3:14

But for those who do not reveal a new heart life, Paul gave a serious warning:

> But if any person's work is burned up [under the test], he will suffer the loss [of it all, losing his reward], though he himself will be saved, but only as [one who has passed] through fire. Do you not discern and understand that you [the whole church at Corinth] are God's temple (His sanctuary), and that God's Spirit has His permanent dwelling in you [to be at home in you, collectively as a church and also individually]?
>
> —1 CORINTHIANS 3:15–16

We will be tested. This is God's "checks-and-balance" way of seeing what rules in our lives. Is it your mind or your heart? I believe the test determines which part of you is in control. Do the thought patterns of your mind, which say "Fight back," "Be jealous" or "Be envious," determine your response? If so, you have reacted from your flesh and have sown to the fleshly realm, which is your mind, soul and body.

Or does your new heart overrule the old thought patterns? If your new heart controls your response, you have come out of the fire walking in the Spirit. You are truly minding the things of the Spirit.

Meditation and Renewal

If you simply *read* the Word, it will travel through the first, second and third regions of your mind. In order for it to penetrate the fourth center, the frontal lobes, you have to *meditate* on the Word—consistently keep it there until it permeates the fourth realm of decision. Then, as you study the Word, it will travel down your nerve endings and cause your body functions to relax and line up with the will of God.

As you keep putting the Word inside of you, it will pierce on the subconscious level and begin to heal your emotional memories. Then you will be able to stop comparing against negative, *emotionally familiar* experiences. As the Word pierces the depths of your mind, it will compare and replace these old memories according to the Word of God. You will gain a new perspective—one that will amaze you. Instead of being tormented by your old mind, you will be able to say, "No, I want the Word."

You have to keep meditating on the Word day and night (Ps. 1:2). Digest the Word over and over again until it gets through the cerebral cortex where you think, strategize, plan, reflect and become inspired as God takes your vision for the future to an incredible, new level. Then your imagination takes over from there, and you start seeing yourself succeed and prosper—until you have become an overcomer! As you consistently meditate on the Word, it will go to the frontal lobes, where the power of your decision will declare, "As for me and my house, we are going to live for God!"

David knew the power of meditating on God's Word. He said:

> Your word have I laid up in my heart, that I might not sin against You.
>
> —PSALM 119:11

In Romans 12:2, Paul added, "Do not be conformed to this world...but be transformed...by the [entire] renewal of your mind [by its new ideals and its new attitude], so that you may prove [for yourselves] what is the good and acceptable and perfect will of God." The "[entire] renewal of your mind" will lead you through a transformation in all four regions of your brain.

I believe that when you receive the new heart, its power breaks the shackles of things that possessed you as a sinner (things that you hated and denounced). Yet there are still things that you love and do not want to release. Then it becomes the power of your decision to surrender those things to the Lord, which is done during your mind's *renewing* process. This is the first level—confronting the old habits (those things you love) just as God confronted me in Chicago.

Take cigarette smoking, for example. Though your heart has been converted, your mind still wants a cigarette. It wants that old habit. Therefore, it has to go through the four stages of deliverance by way of the Word.

Deliverance Step by Step

Let's investigate each step. The medulla, which contains the nerve centers that regulate breathing, heart rate and other body functions, begins to get taken care of at conversion. It starts to regulate and balance. The second stage involves the amygdala (storehouse of emotional memory), comparing the new information with what your emotions have already experienced. This is where the new heart information says, "I do not want to smoke. I want God. I live for God…" There has to be a showdown between the new heart and the old mind, which is where your internal battle begins.

When you begin to read the Word of God, the pressure waves from your new heart become so powerful that your heart rejects what is stored in your mind (in the amygdala). The warfare that comes back to the mind is so powerful that it causes you to get in the Word to see what the Bible says about it. When that Word comes in contact with your emotional memories, it begins to cancel that "smoking memory" and replace it with the new, sanctified thought pattern from your new heart.

> When you receive the new heart, its power breaks the shackles of things that possessed you as a sinner.

Now your new heart is refusing to give up, because it cannot be overthrown. It is, after all, the heart of God. So it presses through to the third realm, the cerebral cortex, where it thinks, strategizes, reasons, plans and inspires, and it causes the brain to imagine what it is like not to smoke. It causes that brain to plan, strategize and be inspired to live for God. How does it do this?

It uses the Word to inspire the mind! It dissects

the Word in order to strategize how you are going to keep your mind stayed on God. This reaches the frontal lobes, which are involved in decision making. You decide, "I am not going to do this anymore," and say "My response to this cigarette is *no!* " The lobes then send waves back to the amygdala to reflect the appropriate emotional response.

Your new heart exerts pressure on the old brain to receive and digest the Word. It goes completely through all four stages. By the time the Word reaches the decision-making center, it has rejected the memory and inspired the mind. After the decision is followed through, the body begins to line up in sync with the new heart rhythms that have passed through the frontal lobes back to the amygdala. This completed process is transmitted back to your physical being through the medulla as it pierces on the subconscious level.

When you begin to read the Word of God, the pressure waves from your new heart become so powerful that your heart rejects what is stored in your mind.

Let's relate this to church. Your body goes to services because your new heart is overpowering the mind. It has divorced the mind and linked up with the heart to say, "I am going to church." The problem is that although many people have allowed their new hearts to exert the control necessary to get their bodies to church, their minds still sit in the pews unresponsively. The purpose for going to church should be to get the Word of God into the four sections of the mind, allowing the mind to reach the point of decision!

Which stage of mind renewal describes where you are today? Is your mind being renewed?

Are you working out your own salvation with fear and trembling before God?

Have you embraced your new heart?

Chapter 10

Rejection of the
New Heart

A new heart comes with many godly attributes, including a strong conviction of what it believes. God already "believes, accepts and receives" Himself. He has every confidence that His Word is true. He knows it will accomplish His divine purpose. (See Isaiah 55:11.) We fall into error when we think of ourselves "more highly" than we should and then fail to trust and obey God. Isaiah 55:7–9 says:

> Let the wicked forsake his way and the unrighteous man his thoughts; and let him return to the Lord, and He will have love, pity, and mercy for him, and to our God, for He will multiply to him His abundant pardon. For My thoughts are not your thoughts, neither are your ways My ways, says the Lord. For as the heavens are higher than the earth, so are My ways higher than your ways and My thoughts than your thoughts.

Many in the church do not have the mind of Christ, so they live in a perpetual state of sin, saying,

"I do not feel convicted about this. I do not feel bad about that." Their consciences have become darkened, and they habitually do things that displease God. They do not love God or fear Him unto obedience. If this describes you, then I am sorry. You do not have the new heart.

When you have the new heart—*God's heart*—and you do anything that is contrary to God's Word, it will automatically send a wave of conviction. And because you love and fear God and believe in His name, you will repent.

> He who believes in Him [who clings to, trusts in, relies on Him] is not judged [he who trusts in Him never comes up for judgment; for him there is no rejection, no condemnation—he incurs no damnation]; but he who does not believe (cleave to, rely on, trust in Him) is judged already [he has already been convicted and has already received his sentence] because he has not believed in and trusted in the name of the only begotten Son of God. [He is condemned for refusing to let his trust rest in Christ's name.] The [basis of the] judgment (indictment, the test by which men are judged, the ground for the sentence) lies in this: the Light has come into the world, and people have loved the darkness rather than and more than the Light, for their works (deeds) were evil. For every wrongdoer hates (loathes, detests) the Light, and will not come out into the Light but shrinks from it, lest his works (his deeds, his activities, his conduct) be exposed and reproved.
>
> —JOHN 3:18–20

There is a penalty for sin, one way or the other. If you habitually do things that are ungodly and sense no conviction, but just say, "God understands," the old heart has deceived you. You are walking out a death sentence. *Remember*:

> The heart is deceitful above all things, and it is exceedingly perverse and corrupt and severely, mortally sick! Who can know it [perceive, understand, be acquainted with his own heart and mind]? I the Lord search the mind, I try the heart, even to give to every man according to his ways, according to the fruit of his doings.
>
> —JEREMIAH 17:9–10

If you can continue in a pattern of sin, you have not received the new heart. The new heart changes you completely, even if you cannot explain it. You cannot "coin" the new birth experience any more than a person can explain exactly what happens when he has undergone a heart transplant. Jesus said:

> The wind blows (breathes) where it wills; and though you hear its sound, yet you neither know where it comes from nor where it is going. So it is with everyone who is born of the Spirit.
>
> —JOHN 3:8

The little girl in chapter seven could not explain why she kept seeing a murder after she received a heart transplant. The older man could not explain why he kept dreaming about a young woman who fell down a flight of stairs.

The new heart is a miracle. I cannot explain how I stopped doing certain things or exactly how I got the victory in some areas. I cannot explain why I am a "new creation," but the Holy Spirit has led me every step of the way. God put a new heart inside of me, and I have never been the same.

Your heart will always tell you who your father is and from where your motivations come.

God's new heart comes with divine passion for the things of the Spirit. The new heart craves what God craves, loves what He loves and hates what He hates. So how is it that we can say we have received the heart of God, yet we do not love what God loves, we do not hate what He hates or we do not crave after righteousness as He does?

If you do not love God or fear Him unto obedience, you do not have the new heart.

When we receive God's heart, it should birth a passion within us for holiness, worship and everything that pleases Him. It should automatically reject anything that does not sound, look, taste or feel like God. If it does not do this, something is wrong.

The Word says that we have been made "the righteousness of God in him" (2 Cor. 5:21, KJV). Unless we train our minds (and, as a result, our flesh) to line up with who we have already become, we will fall into deception.

In the Garden of Gethsemane, Jesus said this: "My Father, if it is possible, let this cup pass away from Me" (Matt. 26:39). At that moment, Jesus' mind was fighting the warfare for what His physical body would soon have to endure, so that He would be able to fulfill the assignment of His new heart.

If Jesus had disobeyed the Father and rejected His new heart, God's eternal plan would not have been fulfilled—and His new heart would have died (just as a natural heart's signal is cut off by constant refusals from the brain). This is how a person falls into a backslidden state. The new heart says, "Do not do this." But the mind refuses over and over again, saying, "I am going to do what I want."

The Danger of Habitual Sin

When you reject the Word and do not put it into your heart and mind, the old nature assumes control—and you shut down the power and the activity of your new heart. God will not stay in this temple. You will have forced the Holy Spirit to leave, and not because you have done "one little thing" wrong. He will have left because you have refused to store the Word of God in your mind, enabling it to progress through all four stages of deliverance. You have refused to meditate on the Word. Therefore, your "emotional memories" and the stubbornness of your old mind can draw your heart to do something that offends God.

Anyone can make a mistake. Falling into temptation and sin does not mean that you are not saved. But when ungodly behavior becomes habitual to the point that you no longer sense the heart's conviction, the new heart has been repelled. Because you have ignored the new heart's correction—deliberately annihilating its message, which says that you no longer desire God—you have rejected your new heart. To consistently refuse the new heart's direction, you are sending a signal back saying, "I do not want you here." And the Spirit of the Lord will never stay where He is not wanted.

Overtaken in Sin, or a Reprobate Mind?

If you allow your flesh (mind) to lead you into sin, and then you repent, God is just and able to forgive you. Why? You have been overtaken in a fault. Overtaken by what? You have been overtaken by memories of the brain. Man looks on the outside, but God sees your heart (1 Sam. 16:7). He knows that sin action did not come from your heart. It cropped up from your emotional memories. This is why it is critical for you to renew your mind.

In all his victories through the help he received from the Lord, King Uzziah had become a mighty ruler. Scripture says, "As long as he sought (inquired of, yearned for) the Lord, God made him prosper" (2 Chron. 26:5). As king, Uzziah "did right in the Lord's sight," until he began to think "too highly" of himself, thus usurping God's established authority in the priesthood.

Uzziah had become wealthy, strong and famous. Obviously, he had started to believe that nothing was impossible to him—even if it perverted God's ways. This is where his heart deceived him. As king, he should have recognized the Torah as God's final authority. As a "son," he should have humbled himself under God's mighty hand—but his heart had become filled with pride. Uzziah forced his way into the temple to offer incense despite the priests' strong objections, and God struck him with leprosy. (See 2 Chronicles 26:16–19.) Uzziah was deceived by powerful emotional memories, which led to his greatest—and final—defeat.

When God turns someone over to a "reprobate" mind, more often than not it is someone who has declared that he has a new heart. Although that person receives convicting messages from God, he ignores them…*continuously*. His actions become a mockery against God. God has no other choice but to turn that person over to a reprobate mind.

> And even as they did not like to retain God in their knowledge, God gave them over to a reprobate mind, to do those things which are not convenient.
>
> —ROMANS 1:28, KJV

Saul was crowned the first king of Israel. Very tall and handsome, he had probably become accustomed to being the center of attention—and he was, until he sinned against God. A young shepherd boy became his most influential protégé. David served Saul with all of his heart and received great favor from the Lord. Yet because Saul was a "man of the people," he grew more and more jealous of David— to the point that he relentlessly hunted him down like a wild animal.

God had already stripped Saul of his kingly authority, but instead of repenting, Saul used every ounce of his power to save face before the people over and over again. His actions and condition kept getting worse. He lied, murdered and manipulated—all while putting on the "form" of kingship and royalty! God turned him over to his wicked thoughts, and the man who had begun his reign by prophesying with the prophets ended up seeking psychics and dying at the hands of his enemies. (See 1 Samuel 9–31.)

Uzziah was deceived by powerful emotional memories, which led to his greatest—and final—defeat.

This is the danger that faces the church today. Many people are still saying, "I am saved," as they willfully and continually do things that displease God. That offends Him, to the point that He turns them over to a deceived and debased mind. This kind of mind is "deceitful...perverse...corrupt...and severely, mortally sick."

It would be better for these people to say, "I was saved, but I am in a backslidden state right now. I need prayer. My memories remind me what it felt like to be in an adulterous situation, and I just cannot say *no* to my brainwaves. The memory is too strong. I cannot overthrow it." There is grace and mercy for these individuals. But when you have a new heart (that constantly sends waves of conviction), and you constantly reject the conviction while declaring how righteous and holy you are, the Spirit of the Lord will leave...just as He left Saul.

> For if anyone only listens to the Word without obeying it and being a doer of it, he is like a man who looks carefully at his [own] natural face in a mirror; for he thoughtfully observes himself, and then goes off and promptly forgets what he was like.
>
> —JAMES 1:23–24

They are committing spiritual suicide by willingly "putting to death" the "breath of life" that God has sovereignly placed in their hearts. They know the truth, but over and over again they reject it. Then they walk away and pretend that everything is OK. This leaves God with no alternative.

The New **Evil** Heart

As we learned in chapter six, when we have the new heart and are studying the Word consistently, we have the ability to "squeeze out" ungodly thought patterns. If we refuse to accept the directions of God's Word and act upon that evil thought, God has no alternative but to leave. He cannot dwell in the same place as sin.

This puts you in imminent danger. When you backslide, your latter state becomes worse than your original state before receiving the new heart. Therefore, you will begin to experience the depths of the evil realm, which is worse than you have ever dreamed. Hear me. If you have followed the command of Joel 2:12–13 to rip out your old heart, and God has given you a new heart according to Ezekiel 11:19–20, and yet you reject that new heart, you will not merely revert back to the old heart that you had before.

You will receive another heart from Satan, one that is prepared to receive seven times the amount of evil that you once held in your old heart. This "evil" heart will also not connect to your nerve endings, so you could end up becoming a murderer! As the evil battle begins, your old mind may say, "I have never killed anybody before." But the evil heart you have received from Satan has also come programmed with an assignment for evil—and you will end up doing evil and wicked things that you never dreamed you would do.

When you tear up and rip out your old heart, the Bible says that God casts it into the depths of the sea (Mic. 7:19). He removes it from you as far as the east is from the west, so you cannot go back and get that old heart (Ps. 103:12). When you backslide, leave God and say, "I do not want to hear the Word of God. I do not want to transform my mind so that it can line up with my new heart," then you do not get your old heart back! It has been cast into outer darkness. It is gone!

When you reject God, Satan brings you an evil heart, and you do not know what is in that heart, either. It is even more deceitful, because it "looks like" it is in perfect order—until it begins its evil transformation.

> When the strong man, fully armed, [from his courtyard] guards his own dwelling, his belongings are undisturbed [his property is at peace and is secure]. But when one stronger than he attacks him and conquers him, he robs him of his whole armor on which he had relied and divides up and distributes all his

goods as plunder (spoil). He who is not with Me [siding and believing with Me] is against Me, and he who does not gather with Me [engage in My interest], scatters. When the unclean spirit has gone out of a person, it roams through waterless places in search [of a place] of rest (release, refreshment, ease); and finding none it says, I will go back to my house from which I came. And when it arrives, it finds [the place] swept and put in order and furnished and decorated. And it goes and brings other spirits [seven of them], more evil than itself, and they enter in, settle down, and dwell there; and the last state of that person is worse than the first.

—LUKE 11:21–26

Like the first heart transplant, your evil heart will not be connected to your mind. It will not obey you, either.

When you "rend your heart" and give it to God, do you think that He puts it in a bank account and saves it? Do you think that He puts it in cold storage, saying "I will save it just in case you do not want Me later?" No! He destroys it, just like anything else that looks like death. The destiny of that old heart is death and destruction, and since He came to give us everlasting, abundant life, He destroys anything that resembles death. God does not save "death."

"Hearken" to (hear intelligently) the Word of the Lord in this matter. God is sending this Word because we do not realize just how powerful backsliding is! The very reason we get rid of the old heart (the one "housed" in our life until we become saved) is because it is too dangerous to hold on to (because, "Who can know it?"). If you cannot know that heart,

how will you ever know the one that Satan brings—
one seven times worse than the first one?

This ought to make you hold on to God even if you
have to fight tooth and nail. This knowledge should
make you determined to put your old mind to death.
It should make you feed your mind with the Word of
God *every day*, because you do not ever want to
backslide.

Spiritually, the only difference is this: Satan already has donors lined up. *He is ready*.

When a surgeon takes out an old, damaged heart
he does not try to restore it. He discards it. (God is
trying to tell us something. He is trying to show us
through medical science, again, what His process
is!) If your body rejects your new heart, the doctors
would never go back and get your old one. They
couldn't—it is gone! So they would put your name
back on the list to receive a second new heart, and
you would have wait for another donor. Spiritually,
the only difference is this: Satan already has donors
lined up. *He is ready*.

A Deadly Disease

After you have received a new heart (and new
blood), if you "quench the Spirit," rejecting God,
you might as well have injected poison into your

veins. It could be likened to contracting AIDS, which starts to kill your immune system. It travels to the weakest part of your body and starts attacking that area. When that poison starts hitting your blood (because you have rejected the Word of God), you will begin to experience a full AIDS manifestation. And it will kill you.

AIDS usually starts by infecting the lungs, where the "breath of life" keeps oxygen flowing through a person's body. When he can no longer breathe, his lungs fill up with fluid, pneumonia sets in and his condition becomes critical. At this stage (in the spirit realm), he starts to "drop weight" and slowly begins to lose power—his punch, kick and overall strength. The enemy is destroying his "breath of life."

A Fatal Attack

At one time, my pastor was eating things that were unhealthy for his body. The arteries leading to his heart became clogged because of things he had eaten (that his mind had told him he should have). This was not his heart's desire. His *mind* said, "I want bacon." Did his heart completely fail him? No. He had a stroke, so there was nothing wrong with his heart. Yet there was something wrong with the artery that led to his heart.

When people fall into temptation, it does not mean their hearts are messed up. They have had a spiritual stroke. The artery can be unclogged through spiritual surgery according to the Word of God. The valve can be restored so that the blood can continue to flow to the heart. Only the blood can wash and make you clean and keep that new heart purified. This same blood flows to the heart and goes back up to the brain with oxygen so that the brain is able to think clearly again.

When a doctor tells his patient what to do in order to stay healthy, and she refuses to obey his orders, eating everything that she can get her hands on, it will ultimately affect her heart. If she has a stroke, she can become paralyzed and possibly lose the ability to think clearly, move or talk. Her body and face could become twisted and distorted. On the spiritual side, this means she would no longer resemble Christ.

This same blood flows to the heart and goes back up to the brain with oxygen so the brain is able to think clearly again.

Some people are paralyzed for life due to a physical stroke. In the spirit realm, this is why some people sit in church unable to lift up their hands! They cannot dance, sing or worship because they have suffered a stroke. The heart is still intact, but the stroke indicates that unhealthy things have been put into their bodies. Thus the new heart rejects that polluted blood. If their arteries remain clogged and they do not change, a spiritual heart attack could kill them.

The Time for Change Has Come

God is saying, loud and clear, that if we intend to live throughout eternity—if we intend to live for Him in this world—we need to change. If we don't, we will have massive heart failure and die a spiritual death. This is definitely a *matter of the heart*. Proverbs 4:23 says, "Keep and guard your heart with all vigilance and above all that you guard, for out of it flow the springs of life."

We must be vigilant, constantly examining our own hearts. Otherwise, we will continue to be the "great pretenders." One day the Lord may say to us, "Begone from Me...I never knew you" (Matt. 25:41; 7:23).

The Word of the Lord speaks to us from Revelation 2:5:

> Remember then from what heights you have fallen. Repent (change the inner man to meet God's will) and do the works you did previously [when first you knew the Lord].

As I close this chapter, heed this warning to care for your new heart diligently. Follow this advice from 2 Corinthians 13:5–11:

> Examine and test and evaluate your own selves to see whether you are holding to your faith and showing the proper fruits of it. Test and prove yourselves [not Christ]. Do you not yourselves realize and know [thoroughly by an ever-increasing experience] that Jesus Christ is in you—unless you are [counterfeits] disapproved on trial and rejected? But I hope you

will recognize and know that we are not disapproved on trial and rejected. But I pray to God that you may do nothing wrong, not in order that we [our teaching] may appear to be approved, but that you may continue doing right...

For we can do nothing against the Truth [not serve any party or personal interest], but only for the Truth [which is the Gospel]...And this we also pray for: your all-round strengthening and perfecting of soul. So I write these things while I am absent from you, that when I come to you, I may not have to deal sharply in my use of the authority which the Lord has given me [to be employed, however] for building [you] up and not for tearing [you] down.

Finally, brethren, farewell (rejoice)! Be strengthened (perfected, completed, made what you ought to be); be encouraged and consoled and comforted; be of the same [agreeable] mind one with another; live in peace, and [then] the God of love [Who is the Source of affection, goodwill, love, and benevolence toward men] and the Author and Promoter of peace will be with you.

God will be with us if we trust and obey our new heart. Above anything else, we must know that *we have it*.

Chapter 11

Prayer **Keys**

We know the problem, we have read the prophetic word, and we have examined the depths of the heart and mind. Now it's time to put what we know into practice. It's time to take the *keys* of God's Word and, from the deep chambers of our hearts, unshackle our minds—and ultimately the world—from the enemy's bondage. Remember what Jesus said in Matthew 16:19:

> I will give you the keys of the kingdom of heaven; and whatever you bind (declare to be improper and unlawful) on earth must be what is already bound in heaven; and whatever you loose (declare lawful) on earth must be what is already loosed in heaven.

We are to "bind" what God has already bound in His Word and to "loose" what He has already loosed. We are not supposed to bind and loose what we desire or anything that has not first been revealed to us by God. If we have received the new heart, both heart and mind should be totally submitted to God's Word and ways. This is how we begin to experience and walk in the "counsel" of God.

Blessed (happy, fortunate, prosperous, and envi-
able) is the man who walks and lives not in the
counsel of the ungodly [following their advice,
their plans and purposes], nor stands [submis-
sive and inactive] in the path where sinners
walk, nor sits down [to relax and rest] where the
scornful [and the mockers] gather. But his
delight and desire are in the law of the Lord, and
on His law (the precepts, the instructions, the
teachings of God) he habitually meditates (pon-
ders and studies) by day and by night. And he
shall be like a tree firmly planted [and tended]
by the streams of water, ready to bring forth its
fruit in its season; its leaf also shall not fade or
wither; and everything he does shall prosper
[and come to maturity].

—PSALM 1:1–3

God is saying that we are to break old, fleshly
habits and build a new habit of meditating on His
Word…day and night. Let me bring this down to
earth. It takes about twenty-one days to establish a
new habit in your mind. So why don't you challenge
yourself—for the next twenty-one days—to study
and ponder the Word of God day and night? You will
get results…and your battle will be won. When
Daniel sought God for a message, the angel appeared
and told him:

Fear not, Daniel, for from the first day that you
set your mind and heart to understand and to
humble yourself before your God, your words
were heard, and I have come as a consequence
of [and in response to] your words. But the
prince of the kingdom of Persia withstood me
for twenty-one days. Then Michael, one of the
chief [of the celestial] princes, came to help me,

for I remained there with the kings of Persia.
Now I have come to make you understand what
is to befall your people in the latter days, for the
vision is for [many] days yet to come.
—DANIEL 10:12–14

This could not be a coincidence! If you want to
change, you have to "sow to the Spirit," consistently
and persistently, to complete the transformation
according to God's Word. That is when understanding comes. This is what God is after. This is what
God wants to "unlock" through your new heart in
order to renew your mind.

In Hebrews 4:12 we discover that an understanding of God's Word is released through our heart,
which pierces the brainwaves and flows through our
emotions to transform our thoughts, plans and imagination. We read:

> For the Word that God speaks is alive and full of
> power [making it active, operative, energizing,
> and effective]; it is sharper than any two-edged
> sword, penetrating to the dividing line of the
> breath of life (soul) and [the immortal] spirit,
> and of joints and marrow [of the deepest parts
> of our nature], exposing and sifting and analyz-
> ing and judging the very thoughts and purposes
> of the heart.

Based on this verse, you *decide* to obey the Word,
and your brainwaves flow back through your emotions
to your body and into the depths of your subconscious
mind. The transformation is complete: soul, spirit,
joints and marrow.

As you seek God in prayer, the Holy Spirit will
begin to lead you into the counsel of God's Word.

When you hear the voice of God in prayer, He will either speak to you through His Word (using His Word) or by speaking in harmony with what He has already revealed. The more you seek God, the deeper His counsel will become, and the more "secrets" He will reveal. You will gain more and more understanding. James 1:5–8 says:

> If any of you is deficient in wisdom, let him ask of the giving God [Who gives] to everyone liberally and ungrudgingly, without reproaching or faultfinding, and it will be given him. Only it must be in faith that he asks with no wavering (no hesitating, no doubting). For the one who wavers (hesitates, doubts) is like the billowing surge out at sea that is blown hither and thither and tossed by the wind. For truly, let not such a person imagine that he will receive anything [he asks for] from the Lord, [for being as he is] a man of two minds (hesitating, dubious, irresolute), [he is] unstable and unreliable and uncertain about everything [he thinks, feels, decides].

Being *double-minded* is a state of conflict between the "brain of the heart" and the brain in your head. It is spiritual schizophrenia! It is proof that your new heart is still fighting for the victory. So how do you identify the wisdom that comes from God?

> But the wisdom from above is first of all pure (undefiled); then it is peace-loving, courteous (considerate, gentle). [It is willing to] yield to reason, full of compassion and good fruits; it is wholehearted and straightforward, impartial and unfeigned (free from doubts, wavering, and insincerity).
>
> —JAMES 3:17

When you respond to your new heart, obeying its "intelligent communication" so that the Word penetrates your mind and brings your body into subjection to God's Word, you have won the victory.

> Who is the man who reverently fears and worships the Lord? Him shall He teach in the way that he should choose. He himself shall dwell at ease, and his offspring shall inherit the land. The secret [of the sweet, satisfying companionship] of the Lord have they who fear (revere and worship) Him, and He will show them His covenant and reveal to them its [deep, inner] meaning.
>
> —PSALM 25:12–14

Once you have gained the victory of the new heart, you can consistently receive and respond to the undefiled wisdom of our Father. He can trust you with His secrets.

If you are living in sin, the only thing that God will likely tell you is to repent. Once you have repented from habitual sin, you can then receive the "deep, inner" meaning of His heavenly counsel.

Sometimes you will receive wisdom in prayer that conflicts with everything you see and feel, but it covers you like a warm blanket. This is the wisdom of God. As you go deeper in God, He will begin to lead you in everything you do. He will give you intercessory "assignments" and tell you what to pray according to His Word. Other times, He will lead you to lie silently at the altar or to dance and sing before Him. The most important thing is to do what He leads you to do and to remember what He has already said.

Write the vision and engrave it so plainly upon
tablets that everyone who passes may [be able
to] read [it easily and quickly] as he hastens by.
For the vision is yet for an appointed time and
it hastens to the end [fulfillment]; it will not
deceive or disappoint. Though it tarry, wait
[earnestly] for it, because it will surely come; it
will not be behindhand on its appointed day.

—HABAKKUK 2:2–3

Once you have repented from habitual sin, you can then receive the "deep, inner" meaning of His heavenly counsel.

If you do not have one already, it is time to start
keeping a prayer journal. Make sure that you write
the day, date and time (and sometimes even the
place) when God speaks to you. Write the scriptures
that He reveals to you. Sometimes He will give you a
verse that describes a problem. When this happens,
ask Him to reveal how you can intercede for His
solution. He will show you. It is always His will for
the power of sin to be broken so that His people can
be delivered from bondage.

Seek, inquire for, and require the Lord while He
may be found [claiming Him by necessity and
by right]; call upon Him while He is near. Let
the wicked forsake his way and the unrighteous
man his thoughts; and let him return to the
Lord, and He will have love, pity, and mercy for

him, and to our God, for He will multiply to him
His abundant pardon…For you shall go out
[from the spiritual exile caused by sin and evil
into the homeland] with joy and be led forth
[by your Leader, the Lord Himself, and His
word] with peace; the mountains and the hills
shall break forth before you into singing, and all
the trees of the field shall clap their hands.
Instead of the thorn shall come up the cypress
tree, and instead of the brier shall come up the
myrtle tree; and it shall be to the Lord for a
name of renown, for an everlasting sign [of jubi-
lant exaltation] and memorial [to His praise],
which shall not be cut off.

—Isaiah 55:6–7, 12–13

God wants to "heal our land" (2 Chron. 7:14). He
longs to deliver us from the problem that has emerged
from our old, deceitful hearts (Jer. 17:9). Yes, we have
been deceived to the point that we have fallen into a
pattern of sin that threatens to paralyze the church if
we do not turn to God and sincerely repent.

We must receive the new heart and begin to seek
God while He can still be found. We must forsake our
own thoughts and put on the humble mind of Christ.
(See Philippians 2:5–8.) Then, and only then, will
God release true "prosperity." And it will not only
heal us; it will heal our land.

Principles of Prayer and Intercession

Before you can begin to pray effectively, you need to
understand exactly what prayer is, so let us begin
with *praise* and *petition*. Yes, I started with praise,

and, yes, it works together with petition! You enter God's presence through your praises, because thanking God proves your faith in Him to perform His Word. After all, if you do not believe that God answers prayer, you might as well not even ask—because He does not answer "double-minded" requests. Philippians 4:6–7 says:

> Do not fret or have any anxiety about anything, but in every circumstance and in everything, by prayer and petition (definite requests), with thanksgiving, continue to make your wants known to God. And God's peace [shall be yours, that tranquil state of a soul assured of its salvation through Christ, and so fearing nothing from God and being content with its earthly lot of whatever sort that is, that peace] which transcends all understanding shall garrison and mount guard over your hearts and minds in Christ Jesus.

There is also an intensified prayer of *consecration* where you press into God with a need to know or to do God's will. (See Matthew 26:39.) Another type of prayer is the prayer of *faith*, or an urgent request for God to intervene in a situation that usually requires an immediate answer. (See James 5:15.) The prayer of *agreement* is joining your faith with two or three others before God. (See Matthew 18:19–20.) Finally, *intercession* is when you pray and believe for someone else. (See Isaiah 59:16.)

According to Matthew 7:7–8, there are also levels (or increasing intensities) of prayer:

> Keep on *asking* and it will be given you; keep on *seeking* and you will find; keep on *knocking*

[reverently] and [the door] will be opened to
you. For everyone who keeps on asking
receives; and he who keeps on seeking finds;
and to him who keeps on knocking, [the door]
will be opened.

—EMPHASIS ADDED

The kingdom of God is like "something precious
buried in a field" (Matt. 13:44). Sometimes we have to
dig deeper, wait longer and press in harder to get the
full revelation.

Simply put, to *ask* is to petition God for your
needs or to intercede for the needs of others. To seek
means to ask God for deeper wisdom and, at the
same time, to search the Word for deeper insight.
Seeking can also mean that you study other
resources or look more deeply into the things
around you. It can also mean that you receive godly
counsel in order to get a full understanding of what
God is saying.

Knocking is pressing in further through persistent
prayer, fasting and obedience to God's revealed and
written Word. When you fast, you willingly give up
food and anything else that stands in God's way in
order to hear God, obey Him and accomplish His
purpose.

[Rather] is not this the fast that I have chosen:
to loose the bonds of wickedness, to undo the
bands of the yoke, to let the oppressed go free,
and that you break every [enslaving] yoke? Is it
not to divide your bread with the hungry and
bring the homeless poor into your house—
when you see the naked, that you cover him,
and that you hide not yourself from [the needs
of] your own flesh and blood?

Then shall your light break forth like the morning, and your healing (your restoration and the power of a new life) shall spring forth speedily; your righteousness (your rightness, your justice, and your right relationship with God) shall go before you [conducting you to peace and prosperity], and the glory of the Lord shall be your rear guard. Then you shall call, and the Lord will answer; you shall cry, and He will say, Here I am. If you take away from your midst yokes of oppression [wherever you find them], the finger pointed in scorn [toward the oppressed or the godly], and every form of false, harsh, unjust and wicked speaking, and if you pour out that with which you sustain your own life for the hungry and satisfy the need of the afflicted, then shall your light rise in darkness, and your obscurity and gloom become like the noonday.

—Isaiah 58:6–10

Fasting from food is extremely powerful because your new heart is bypassing your mind (which is bent on survival) and going directly to your body, which tells the brain, "Man shall not live and be upheld and sustained by bread alone, but by every word that comes forth from the mouth of God" (Matt. 4:4). To coin a phrase, fasting is "putting your body where your heart is" to squeeze out any form of mind control.

This is also why it is good to meditate even more deeply on the Word during a fast. It escalates the two-pronged counterattack (discussed in chapter seven) to an all-out, three-pronged assault against the enemy. In other words, denying yourself food can help you to see that other "earthly" things are not that important—which opens the door to obedience in every area of your life. Ecclesiastes 4:12 says, "A threefold cord is not quickly broken."

To coin a phrase, fasting is "putting your body where your heart is" to squeeze out any form of mind control.

When you overcome in a fast, the devil has to flee; there is a clear path—*within you and outside of you*—for God's will and purpose to be done. Let me say this a different way: When you overcome by denying yourself food, time, money, convenience and whatever you value most, the devil will not be able to tempt you because you have already rejected everything that he can throw in your direction. And he cannot stay in the light; he has to run from it, because his evil deeds are immediately seen and exposed for what they truly are.

Getting to the Heart of Prayer

Obviously, prayer is not what it needs to be in the body of Christ because we are operating from wicked, deceived hearts (Jer. 17:9). Prayer will be restored as we obey our new hearts and renew our old, stubborn minds. Today, in this season and final hour of the church, prayer will be the final test of any genuine believer or work for God:

Dwell in Me, and I will dwell in you. [Live in Me,
and I will live in you.] Just as no branch can
bear fruit of itself without abiding in (being
vitally united to) the vine, neither can you bear
fruit unless you abide in Me. I am the Vine; you
are the branches. Whoever lives in Me and I in
him bears much (abundant) fruit. However,
apart from Me [cut off from vital union with Me]
you can do nothing. If a person does not dwell
in Me, he is thrown out like a [broken-off]
branch, and withers; such branches are gathered up and thrown into the fire, and they are
burned. If you live in Me [abide vitally united to
Me] and My words remain in you and continue
to live in your hearts, ask whatever you will,
and it shall be done for you.

—JOHN 15:4–7

Prayer is our vital connection to God through the
vehicle of our new hearts. If we do not pray, we will
not have the life of Christ within us. We will be unpro-
ductive and, even worse, could be told on that Day, "I
never knew you."

You must decide whether to hear and embrace
this word of prophecy—and inherit eternal life—or
to continue walking in your own thoughts and ways,
and reap destruction. The choice is yours.

I pray and trust that you will choose to obey God
and reap eternal life.

To get you started, the following are a few steps to
develop your daily devotions, as well as a few
Scripture keys on the heart and mind.

The Practice of Prayer

I adapted this daily "prayer practice" from a powerful, in-depth teaching called "The Power of Positive Prayer Points" in Matthew Ashimolowo's special edition Bible.[1]

1. Start each day loving God and people. This means your relationship with God is good, and that as far as you are able, your relationships with family members, friends, coworkers and others are in line with the Word.

2. Start each day communing with God through Bible study and prayer.

3. Thank God, praise Him for answering your prayers and worship Him for who He is.

4. Repent, asking God to forgive you and to cleanse your heart from every sin, known and unknown.

5. Thank God for your spiritual armor, as listed in Ephesians 6:10–18.

6. Surrender yourself to the Holy Spirit so He can pray through you, according to Romans 8:26–27.

7. Be ready to obey the Holy Spirit's leading, to petition (for your needs) or intercede (for others); declare God's

Word; lie still, or do whatever God leads you to do.

8.   Ask God to build a hedge of protection around your life, family and all others who are praying with you against the enemy's devices.

9.   Ask God to rebuke Satan and all his servants.

10. Take authority over the enemy's work and his attempts to attack your new heart (spirit), your mind (emotions, logic, and decision making) and body.

11. Repeat these steps until you know that you have broken through in the Spirit realm and that God is leading you in prayer and intercession.

A Few Prayer Keys for the Heart

Here are a few scriptures to get you started as you seek God in prayer daily, learning to embrace your new heart. Put yourself in these scriptures as you meditate on the Word. For example, "I shall love the Lord my God with all my mind and heart..."

> Create in me a clean heart, O God, and renew a right, persevering, and steadfast spirit within me...Let the words of my mouth and the meditation of my heart be acceptable in Your sight,

O Lord, my [firm, impenetrable] Rock and my Redeemer.

—PSALM 51:10; 19:14

A new heart will I give you and a new spirit will I put within you, and I will take away the stony heart out of your flesh and give you a heart of flesh.

—EZEKIEL 36:26

Search me [thoroughly], O God, and know my heart! Try me and know my thoughts! And see if there is any wicked or hurtful way in me, and lead me in the way everlasting.

—PSALM 139:23–24

Teach me Your way, O Lord, that I may walk and live in Your truth; direct and unite my heart [solely, reverently] to fear and honor Your name.

—PSALM 86:11

I delight to do Your will, O my God; yes, Your law is within my heart.

—PSALM 40:8

As for what was sown on good soil, this is he who hears the Word and grasps and comprehends it; he indeed bears fruit and yields in one case a hundred times as much as was sown, in another sixty times as much, and in another thirty.

—MATTHEW 13:23

And you shall love the Lord your God with all your [mind and] heart and with your entire being and with all your might.

—DEUTERONOMY 6:5

A Few Prayer Keys for the Mind

As I was studying, I found that the word *heart* is used at least seven times more in the Bible than the word *mind*. Many of these uses of the word *heart* refer to both heart and mind, but I believe this is because the heart comes first—in the natural and spiritual realms. Begin to meditate on these scriptures:

> For who has known or understood the mind (counsels and purposes) of the Lord so as to guide and instruct Him and give Him knowledge? But we have the mind of Christ (the Messiah) and do hold the thoughts (feelings and purposes) of His heart.
>
> —1 CORINTHIANS 2:16

> Do not be conformed to this world (this age), [fashioned after and adapted to its external, superficial customs], but be transformed (changed) by the [entire] renewal of your mind [by its new ideals and its new attitude], so that you may prove [for yourselves] what is the good and acceptable and perfect will of God, even the thing which is good and acceptable and perfect [in His sight for you].
>
> —ROMANS 12:2

> And be constantly renewed in the spirit of your mind [having a fresh mental and spiritual attitude], and put on the new nature (the regenerate self) created in God's image, [Godlike] in true righteousness and holiness.
>
> —EPHESIANS 4:23–24

You will guard him and keep him in perfect and constant peace whose mind [both its inclination and its character] is stayed on You, because he commits himself to You, leans on You, and hopes confidently in You.

—ISAIAH 26:3

I will imprint My laws upon their minds, even upon their innermost thoughts and understanding, and engrave them upon their hearts; and I will be their God, and they shall be My people.

—HEBREWS 8:10

For God did not give us a spirit of timidity (of cowardice, of craven and cringing and fawning fear), but [He has given us a spirit] of power and of love and of calm and well-balanced mind and discipline and self-control.

—2 TIMOTHY 1:7

So brace up your minds; be sober (circumspect, morally alert); set your hope wholly and unchangeably on the grace (divine favor) that is coming to you when Jesus Christ (the Messiah) is revealed.

—1 PETER 1:13

Again, these verses will get you started. As you continue to seek, study and meditate upon God's Word, He will finish the work that He has started in you.

God Can Still Deliver Us

Yes, the new heart message is a mandate for me to preach, because so many believers have been deceived (as I was) about their own hearts. So many *think* they are saved, but they still do not know Christ. Many leaders and preachers have not yet been born again, or they are not telling the whole truth and causing others to stumble. Yes, knowing Christ has become "unattainable," but God can still deliver us.

God turned me around, so I know that He will do the same for you. Like me, you need to ask God to give you a new heart.

> Therefore also now, says the Lord, turn and keep on coming to Me with all your heart, with fasting, with weeping, and with mourning [until every hindrance is removed and the broken fellowship is restored]. Rend your hearts and not your garments and return to the Lord, your God, for He is gracious and merciful, slow to anger, and abounding in loving-kindness; and He revokes His sentence of evil [when His conditions are met].
>
> —JOEL 2:12–13

It is time to return to the Lord, because nothing is more important than *the matters of the heart.*

Notes

Introduction
How It **All Began**

1. "Give Me a Clean Heart," public domain.

Chapter 1
We Need a **New Heart**

1. James Strong, *The New Strong's Exhaustive Concordance of the Bible,* (Nashville, TN: Thomas Nelson, 1984), s.v. 5315, "soul."
2. Ibid., s.v. 5368, *"phileo."*

Chapter 6
A Scientific **Point of View**

1. Doc Lew Childre and Howard Martin, *The HeartMath Solution* (San Francisco, CA: HarperSanFrancisco, 2000), 9.
2. Ibid., 33.
3. Ibid., 9.
4. Ibid., 32.
5. Ibid., 10.
6. Strong, *The New Strong's Exhaustive Concordance of the Bible,* s.v. 3788, "eye."
7. Ibid., s. v. 573, 4120, "single."
8. Childre and Martin, *The HeartMath Solution*, 31.
9. Ibid., 34.

Chapter 7

Results of a **Heart Transplant**

1. Paul Pearsall, "The Heart That Found Its Body's Killer," *The Heart's Code* (New York: Broadway Books, 1998), 7.
2. *The Art Bell Show* (syndicated), as aired on New Talk Radio, 570 KLIF, Dallas, Texas, March 21, 2002.
3. Pearsall, *The Heart's Code*, 24–25.
4. Childre and Martin, "The Brain in the Heart," *The HeartMath Solution*, 10.
5. Ibid., "Let's Make a Deal," 41.

Chapter 8

The New **Heart**

1. Pearsall, *The Heart's Code*, 66.
2. Childre and Martin, *The HeartMath Solution*, 34.
3. Strong, *The New Strong's Exhaustive Concordance of the Bible*, s.v. 8085, "hearken."

Chapter 9

The Renewed **Mind**

1. Adapted from Childre and Martin, *The HeartMath Solution*, 31.
2. Elaine Farris Hughes, *Writing from the Inner Self* (New York: Harper Perennial, 1992), 4.
3. Childre and Martin, *The HeartMath Solution*. Also, source retrieved from Internet: The High-Performance Mind and encyclopedia.com.

Chapter 11
Prayer **Keys**

1. The Daily Prayer Practice was adapted from a special
    edition King James Bible by Matthew Ashimolowo, in
    a section titled, "The Power of Positive Prayer
    Points," page 17. For more information regarding this
    resource, contact Matthew Ashimolowo Media
    Ministries, London, England, or go to his website at
    www.kicc.org.uk.

Give Me a Clean Heart...

Psalm 51:10

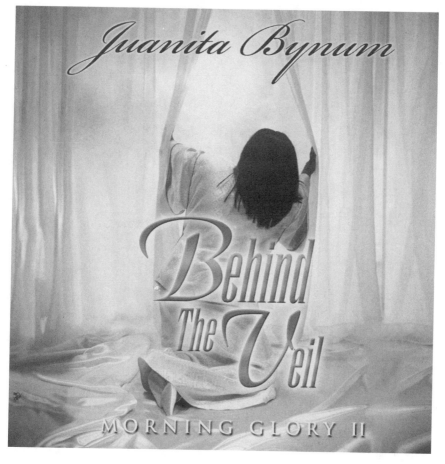

Your Walk With God Can Be Even Deeper...

With *Charisma* magazine, you'll be informed and inspired by the features and stories about what the Holy Spirit is doing in the lives of believers today.

Each issue:

- Brings you exclusive world-wide reports to rejoice over.
- Keeps you informed on the latest news from a Christian perspective.
- Includes miracle-filled testimonies to build your faith.
- Gives you access to relevant teaching and exhortation from the most respected Christian leaders of our day.

Call 1-800-829-3346 for 3 FREE trial issues
Offer #A2CCHB

If you like what you see, then pay the invoice of $22.97 (**saving over 51% off the cover price**) and receive 9 more issues (12 in all). Otherwise, write "cancel" on the invoice, return it, and owe nothing.

Experience the Power of Spirit-Led Living

Charisma Offer #A2CCHB
P.O. Box 420234
Palm Coast, Florida 32142-0234
www.charismamag.com

1884A